How to Eat Brilliantly Every Day

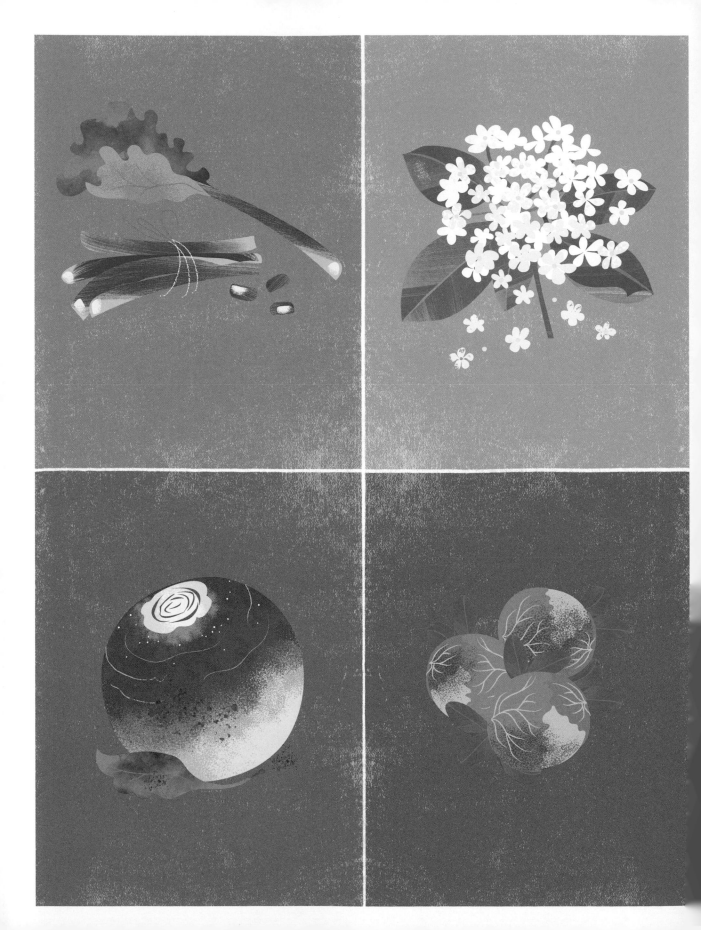

Contents

Introduction

A Potted History of Abel & Cole 6
Why Organic? 7
Our Top Ten Ways to Eat Brilliantly 8
Store Cupboard Swaps 10
Seasonal Swaps: Any Veg'll Do 11

Spring 12

Summer 62

Autumn 132

Winter 198

School of Veg 254

Author Biographies 266
Acknowledgements 267
Index 268

Ⓥ VEGETARIAN Ⓥ VEGAN 🥄 PREP TIME 🍳 COOKING TIME 🍴 SERVINGS ❤ HOW MANY FRUIT OR VEG PORTIONS

A Potted History of Abel & Cole

'Hang on a minute! All potatoes are organic, aren't they? They're vegetables!'
This was Keith Abel back in 1988, where the Abel & Cole story starts. By discovering how
unnecessarily complicated our food systems had become, Keith started to change the way
a few people ate and shopped, and we're still helping people change to this day.

Once upon a time Keith chose potatoes over sitting his bar exams, it was
an unusual decision, but boy, we're glad he made it.

He was going out each day, with his mum and some mates, selling potatoes
door to door, when a farmer told him about this thing called organic.

At the farmer's request, Keith leapt into his rusty old VW and rattled off to Kent.
His jaw nearly touched the dusty ground when he saw inside the spray shed.
It was floor-to-ceiling with bins of chemicals, covered with warning signs.

Keith decided it was time to go back to nature.

He went from offering 'bakers or mashers?' to 'with chemicals or without?'
Not surprisingly, people were keen to hear more.

The early adopters of Abel & Cole joined Keith in his little journey of organic
discovery, learning about all the weird and wonderful veg varieties that come
with working with small-scale organic growers. They swapped the fertilisers,
fungicides, insecticides and pesticides for wonkily seasonal, delicious and
unusual boxes of organic fruit and veg.

For the past 30 years, we've brought the best of our growers' organic fields
to the doorsteps (and tables!) of happy, healthy customers up and down
the country who fancied a change from the usual trolleys and queues.

One of the best bits about organic is that you don't need to be a brilliant cook
to make a stunning meal. The farmer has done a lot of the hard work and the
raw ingredients taste fantastic.

The organic farmers and makers we work with deserve 100 per cent of the
credit for our cooking inspiration. There are a hundred-and-one ways to
serve their much-loved, well-grown food and we've built a bank of organic
food knowhow over the years. We're ridiculously happy to share some of
this knowhow with you here.

Why Organic?

Choose organic and you do more than just avoid pesticide residues.
You're encouraging biodiversity, protecting your countryside (yes, yours!) and all the little things that
rely on it. In fact, you'll be a bit of a hero. We reckon organic food just tastes miles better, too.

Organic produce contains fewer pesticides.

Chemicals such as fungicides, herbicides, and insecticides are widely used
in conventional agriculture, and residues remain on (and in) the food we eat.

Organic food is often fresher.
It has to be, because it
doesn't contain any preservatives to make it last longer. Non-organic
ginger, for instance, can't be used to make homemade ginger beer because
it's undergone ionised radiation in order to increase shelf life and kill any
possible bacteria, but this also destroys its health benefits (and culinary
potential).

Organic farming is better for the environment.

Organic farming practices reduce pollution, conserve water, reduce soil
erosion, increase soil fertility, and use less energy. Farming without
pesticides is also better for nearby birds and animals, as well as people
who live close to farms.

Organic meat means the highest possible welfare standards in the industry.
Organically raised
animals are not routinely fed antibiotics, growth hormones or animal
byprouducts. They're also given more space to move around and more
access to the great outdoors, and a truly natural diet which helps to keep
them healthy.

Organic meat and milk are richer in certain nutrients.
Results from a 2016 European study show that levels of
certain nutrients, including omega-3 fatty acids, were up to 50 per cent
higher in organic meat and milk than in conventionally raised versions.
(Source: British Journal of Nutrition, Cambridge Universiy Press.)

Organic food is GMO-free.
Genetically modified organisms
(GMOs) or genetically engineered (GE) foods are plants whose DNA has
been altered in ways that cannot occur in nature or in traditional
crossbreeding, most commonly in order to be resistant to pesticides or
produce an insecticide.

Our Top Ten Ways to Eat Brilliantly

1 Eat organic. We believe organic is best (that's why we only sell organic food). This is food in its truest form, full of nutrients from healthy soil that hasn't been covered with chemicals. We think it's just a better kind of food and farming. It means cleaner waterways; animals that roam freely in acres of abundant pasture; thriving wildlife and, in some cases, it's healthier for us too. It's good mood food in very many ways.

2 Start with the veg. If you start your meal-planning by putting seasonal veg at the heart of each dish, you'll find you soon pack in the portions without even thinking about it. We do this by using the contents of our weekly veg boxes to inspire our recipes. Soon, you'll be a creative whizz too – check out our School of Veg on pages 254–65 and our simple seasonal swaps on page 10.

3 Go raw. Sometimes not cooking is better than cooking. Even if it's just a quick crunch of a raw carrot at 3pm, or a little salad with each meal, try to wedge in a bit of raw veg each day. A little bit of something raw on every plate will give it freshness, colour and vibrancy.

4 Eat nose-to-tail, veg and all! We never waste anything if we can help it. We love it – it's the most enjoyable (and tastiest) creative challenge ever. Did you know that carrot tops contain six times more vit C than the root? Or that broccoli stalks are full of magnesium? Or chicken livers are a precious source of selenium? Too much food is wasted these days, so be resourceful.

5 Go for fruit. You'll notice a difference when you use seasonal fruit to sweeten puddings and treats. You'll get additional minerals and vitamins and you'll avoid the sugar high-and-low rollercoaster that's hard to get off.

6 Preserve. The magical act of suspending seasonal fruit and veg in time. Jams, pickles, krauts, cordials and more capture the seasons and mean you can have a little bit of summer in winter, and vice versa. Preserving food also helps you waste less. If preserving's really not your bag, then freeze instead. Blanch veg quickly before freezing, and freeze fruit cooked or raw. For more info, have a look at our blog (www.abelandcole.co.uk/blog).

7 Gather wild things. Forage a little and you'll get back to nature as well as finding some free ingredients for your supper. Excellent! Ramble through the woods, walk along the coast, or even stroll through your local park – the great outdoors is brilliant for your wellbeing and wild food can be richer in nutrients than farmed food. Always be sure your collections are not toxic before eating. We have our very own forager who can answer your questions, so just get in touch via our blog (www. abelandcole.co.uk/blog).

8 Try new things and keep learning. Ever swapped peas for kohlrabi? How about baby spinach for wild sea beet? We challenge you to discover something new each month. Be it a variety of apple or cabbage you've never tried, a new cooking technique, or applying a known method to a new ingredient. Be curious and you'll be rewarded. We may even fashion you a trophy out of tofu if you're really adventurous.

9 Be mindful of meat and fish. Sourcing sustainable and ethical meat and fish is a very good idea. Cheap meat and fish means that the animals, people and environment involved get a pretty rough deal. Spend a little more on better meat and fish (ethically, environmentally and quality-ally) and make it go further; have smaller portions and get four meals out of it instead of two; buy less popular (yet still delicious) cuts; or eat meat and fish a little less frequently.

10 Find your healthy balance. Enjoy life, that's our motto. Having a good time is actually more important than lots of very important things. Striking a healthy balance and having a treat after all that veg is a good thing. As they say, a little of what you fancy does you good. In almost all cases.

Store Cupboard Swaps

Some rules are made to be broken and some recipes are open to interpretation. Be creative with veg and fruit, and if you're caught short on store cupboard stuff, use these handy swaps.

INSTEAD OF	AMOUNT	USE
Baking powder	1 tsp	½ tsp bicarbonate of soda
Balsamic vinegar	1 tbsp	1 tbsp any other vinegar + 1 tsp honey/maple syrup
Beer	250ml	250ml cider or white wine
Breadcrumbs	100g	100g blitzed-up oatcakes or crackers
Butter	1 tbsp	1 tbsp olive, rapeseed, sunflower, walnut or coconut oil
Eggs (in baking)	1 egg	50g coconut milk (perfect for vegan baking)
Milk	100ml	75g natural yogurt + 25ml water, or 100ml almond or soy milk
Olive oil	1 tbsp	1 tbsp rapeseed, sunflower, walnut or coconut oil or butter
Plain white flour	100g	85g wholegrain flour
Tomato puree	1 tbsp	4 tbsp tomato sauce or tinned tomatoes boiled until you've got 1 tbsp
Self-raising flour	100g	100g plain white flour + ½ tsp baking powder
Wholegrain flour	100g	100g oats blitzed in a food processor until they resemble flour

Seasonal Swaps: Any Veg'll Do

Eating seasonally means being bold and creative.
In almost all of our recipes you can swap veg and fruit around, depending on what's
in season and what's in your fridge.

Spinach can also mean chard, kale, pak choi, any green cabbage, and even dandelion leaves if you're desperate.

Potatoes can also mean swede, turnips, parsnips, Jerusalem artichokes, beetroot if you fancy a pink plate, or even kohlrabi (sign up to a veg box if you have no idea what that is).

Squash also means pumpkin, sweet potatoes, parsnips, and carrots.

Broccoli means purple sprouting broccoli, asparagus, pears, green beans, runner beans, broad beans – in fact, any green bean. Avoid baked beans: we're not sure that they'd hold up in a stir-fry or soup.

Rocket means watercress, spinach, or lettuce.

Leeks mean onions, shallots, spring onions, garlic, wild garlic, or chives.

Celery can also mean onions, fennel and even celeriac.

Pears can be interchanged with apples.

Plums can become nectarines, peaches or apricots.

Strawberries can also mean blueberries, raspberries or redcurrants, blackcurrants, or gooseberries so long as you add a dash of honey to balance the tartness.

Oranges can also mean tangerines, mandarins, clementines, blood oranges or grapefruit.

SPRING

The first warm days! The blue skies!
Brollies up, brollies down, admire the blossom.
Revel in lighter evenings and go crazy for asparagus and
home-grown rhubarb. Relish the radishes, purple
sprouting broccoli and new season carrots.
Spring is the up beat to our seasonal song.

....

Seasonal Stars

Carrot, cabbage, asparagus, radish, rhubarb, purple
sprouting broccoli, kiwi, banana, passionfruit

....

Jive Time Carrot Mash & Coriander Pesto

Carrot and coriander soup, a classic by any standards. This slightly curried twist is a s-mashingly uplifting side that'll put a spring in your quiff and a boogie in your step.

 V̶ 10 MINS 30 MINS 4 1

750g carrots, peeled and finely diced

4 tbsp olive oil, plus a drop for the carrots

30g fresh coriander

1 small garlic clove

2cm ginger

2cm fresh turmeric (optional)

35g cashews

Sea salt and freshly ground pepper

Pop your carrots in a pot. Add water to a third of the way up the carrots (to steam, not boil them).

Place over a high heat. Add a pinch of salt and a drop of olive oil. Once the water starts to boil, cover and lower the heat a bit.

Cook till tender, about 20 mins. The wider your pan is, the faster your carrots will cook.

Roughly chop the coriander. Peel the garlic, ginger and turmeric (if using). Pile all these ingredients into a food processor or blender. Add the 4 tbsp of oil, the cashews and a pinch of salt. Whizz till smooth, adding a splash of water, if needed, to thin a little.

When the carrots are done, drain them. Mash or whizz in a food processor till smooth. Season with salt and pepper.

Ripple the coriander pesto through the carrots just before serving. Delicious paired with freshly cooked falafel or lamb cutlets.

Za'atar Bazaar

Like couscous if Claude Monet had a go at it. This one's vibrantly colourful, rich with spices and herbs and a good dose of vitamins to boot. You're an artist and your plate is your canvas – go to town.

 15 MINS 5 MINS 4 1

4 large carrots or 1 small bunch with tops

1 garlic clove, grated

3 tbsp sesame seeds

A handful of thyme, leaves only

2 tsp sumac or ground cumin

1 lemon, zest and 2 tbsp + a smack of juice

2 tbsp + a gloss of olive oil

1 red pepper, deseeded and finely diced

Sea salt

If your carrots have tops, trim them. Give both carrots and tops, if using, a good wash. Roughly chop your carrots and put them in a food processor. Blitz till it looks like couscous. No food processor? Simply grate your carrots then finely chop (or just leave them grated).

Finely chop one handful of the carrot tops (you can save the rest of them for stock another day). Fold them through the carrots, along with the garlic.

Set a frying pan over a medium heat. Add your sesame seeds. Toast till just golden – lower the heat if they start to pop and try to escape from the pan.

Mix the toasted sesame seeds with the thyme leaves and the sumac or cumin. Add a pinch of salt. Fold two-thirds of this into your carrot couscous.

Add the lemon zest to the carrot mix. Squeeze 2 tbsp of lemon juice into a jam jar or bowl. Shake (lid on) or whisk with the 2 tbsp of oil and a pinch of salt. Fold through the carrot mix.

Fold the red pepper through the salad. Top with the remaining sesame, thyme and sumac or cumin mix. Taste. Finish with a gloss of oil and another smack of lemon juice, if you like.

Quickle Pickle Carrots, Labneh & Pistou

Waste not, want not (where did I put that soapbox?). This recipe uses every last sliver of the veg, as well as a cheaty homemade cheese. Labneh whey is the hero here; it'll pickle the carrots and their tops to create a stunning dressing to drizzle over the final result. This one's worth the effort.

(V) (⚖) AT LEAST 5 HRS' STRAINING   25 MINS + 1 HR MARINATING + 3 HRS' PICKLING   (🍳) 5 MINS   (🍴) 4   (♡) 1

500g natural yogurt

400g bunched carrots with their tops

1 tbsp honey

1 tsp fennel seeds (optional)

50g cashews

10g basil

2 garlic cloves, roughly chopped

75ml olive oil

1 fennel bulb

Sea salt and freshly ground pepper

To make the labneh, line a sieve with a clean tea towel. Stir the yogurt and 1–2 tsp of salt (depending on taste) together and spoon into the tea towel. Tie the corners up to make a bundle, sit the sieve on a bowl and leave to strain for at least 5 hrs, or ideally overnight in the fridge. (The longer it strains, the thicker and creamier your labneh will be.)

Once the yogurt has drained, you are ready to make the pickled carrots. Slice off the carrot tops and set aside for later. Peel the carrots, then use a vegetable peeler or mandolin to make thin carrot ribbons.

Pour the yogurt whey (the liquid that has drained off) into a bowl. Whisk with the honey and fennel seeds. Toss the carrot ribbons in it. Leave in the fridge to soften for 1 hr.

To make the carrot-top pistou, toast the cashews in a dry frying pan over a medium heat for 2–3 mins till golden. Tip into a food processor.

Plunge the carrot tops and basil sprigs into a pan of boiling water and boil for 5 secs. Drain and sit under cold running water straight away. Shake dry and chuck into the food processor. Add the garlic and the oil. Blitz to make a thick sauce. Taste and season.

Quarter your fennel bulb. Use a veg peeler to make thin, wispy shavings. Toss with the pickled carrots just before serving.

Serve the carrots and fennel with a dollop of labneh. Top with a drizzle of pistou.

Carrot & Cabbage Krautchi

Good for tums and tongues alike. Good for your gut and good for a glut. This Kimchi-Sauerkraut hybrid is incredibly easy and will jazz up all sorts of meals.

 10 MINS, PLUS 2-3 WEEKS' FERMENTING 0 1 LARGE JAR

1 green cabbage

3 carrots

1–2 tbsp grated fresh ginger, depending how gingery you want it (note: you can swap for horseradish if you like)

2 garlic cloves, finely chopped

1 chilli, finely chopped and deseeded

1 tbsp sea salt

Take a couple of the big outer leaves off the cabbage to cover the kraut at the end. Shred the cabbage. Place it in a large glass bowl.

Grate the carrots and add to the cabbage, along with the ginger. Add the garlic and chilli (add less for a milder kick) to the mix along with the salt.

Scrunch everything together with your hands for a few mins, till the veg starts to release some of its juices.

Pack the mixture into a glass jar or crock (about 1.5 to 2 litres). Press firmly down to bring the juices to the top. Cover the mixture with a couple of outer cabbage leaves.

Place a jam jar on top of the cabbage leaf to help weigh it down (put some baking beans or a stone in the jar first to help weigh it down). Cover with a cloth and leave in a dark, warm place for a day.

If, after 24 hours, the liquid that is released does not cover the top of the kraut, make a brine and pour it over the kraut until it is covered.

Let the kraut continue to ferment at room temperature for 5 days, checking it from time to time, ensuring it stays fully covered by the liquid. Smell and taste. Once it's sauerkrauty enough for you, it's ready to eat. Tuck in straight away or store in the fridge in a sealed, sterilised jar till you're ready to eat it. As long as it's covered in brine, it will keep for weeks.

Sing & Kraut

If you need a bit of extra brine in your kraut, simply mix 1 tbsp of sea salt in 1 quart of water. Mix till the salt is completely dissolved. Pour over the kraut till the liquid is above the level of the kraut. For more tips on Kraut, flick through to the School of Veg on page 260.

Greek Slow Roast Hogget Shoulder

Who wants to eat last spring's lamb? You do, and here's why. Hogget's had a longer, richer life with more time to frolic about and develop its taste. Much of the lamb you'll find in shops around this time is imported, which is a bit bonkers when you can get something as gorgeous as this. Beautiful, British and in season.

🔪 15 MINS 🍲 3 HRS 25 MINS, PLUS 30-60 MINS' RESTING 🍴 6

1kg hogget shoulder
1 bulb of garlic
1 lemon
30g fresh oregano
A drop + 2 tbsp of olive oil
1 glass of water or white wine
1 tsp honey (optional)
Sea salt and freshly ground pepper

Preheat your oven to 220°C/Gas 7. Unwrap your meat. Set in a roasting tin. Pat the meat dry. Bring it up to room temperature.

Take a clove from your bulb of garlic. Peel and finely chop. Slice what's left of the garlic bulb in half horizontally. Set aside.

Place the chopped garlic in a pestle and mortar or small bowl. Grate in the zest of the lemon. Add a good pinch of salt and pepper.

Give your oregano a good rinse. Strip the leaves from half the sprigs. Finely chop. Add to the garlic and lemon zest. Muddle it all together with a drop of olive oil, creating a fragrant rub.

Rub half the mix all over your lamb. Reserve a few oregano sprigs for garnishing, and tuck the rest under your lamb. Thinly slice half the lemon. Tuck the slices under your lamb. Nestle the halved garlic bulb under or next to your lamb.

Roast the lamb at the high heat for 25 mins, or till it has a golden crust. Add a glass of water or wine to the tin, cover with a double layer of foil, and lower the heat to 160°C/Gas 3. Roast for 3 hrs.

Add 2 tbsp of the olive oil and 2 tbsp of lemon juice (using your remaining lemon half) to the leftover oregano rub. Whisk till creamy. Taste. Adjust the seasoning and add a little honey, if needed.

Remove the tin from the oven. Unwrap (mind the steam!). Transfer the meat to a cutting board. Rest for 30 mins to 1 hr before carving.

Serve the lemony oregano dressing drizzled over the carved meat. Scatter the leaves from your reserved oregano sprigs over the top.

Griddled Cabbage Steaks with Feta & Mint

We've never met a cabbage we didn't like, although we know how it feels to see a bowling ball-sized head of the stuff monopolising your fridge. This cracker of a cabbage number will use the lot and afterwards you'll wish you had another Goliath stowed away somewhere.

 10 MINS 10 MINS 2 1

1 large green cabbage

A drizzle of olive oil

1 lemon, zest and juice

150g feta

A large handful of mint, leaves only, finely shredded

Freshly ground pepper

Slice your cabbage into 2–3cm thick wedges. These are your steaks. Set a large frying pan over a high heat. Add your cabbage wedges in a single layer – you may need to cook in batches.

Char for about 2 mins on each side (don't add oil to the pan), or till nicely coloured.

Pile onto plates. Finish with a drizzle of olive oil, a grating of lemon zest, a squeeze of lemon juice, crumbled nuggets of feta, the shredded mint leaves and a good pinch of pepper.

Ciderrrr Buttered Greens

We're off to the West Country (without leaving the kitchen, mind) for a spot of simply blanched greens with a splash of the tipple of choice round those parts – cider, of course.

 5 MINS 10 MINS 4 1

4 large handfuls of cabbage or spring greens

50ml cider

1 tbsp butter

A pinch of mixed spice

Sea salt and freshly ground pepper

Bring a large pot of water to the boil. Add a good pinch of salt. Strip out any woody stems from your cabbage or spring greens. Halve, then shred.

Plunge the cabbage into the boiling water. Swirl through. Cook for just 1–2 mins. Drain as soon as the greens are just soft but still a bright, glossy green.

Put your pan back on the heat. Add the cider. Let it boil up and reduce a little. Turn off the heat. Whisk in the butter with a pinch of mixed spice.

Fold the greens through. Season to taste.

Green Kings

Cabbages rule. They're packed with vitamins, high in iron and potassium and low in calories.

To help you love cabbage as much as we do, simply avoid over-cooking. It'll only remind you of school dinners, where cabbage first got a bad name. And you wouldn't want that, would you?

GREEN POINTED (top left)
If it was blue, it would be a Smurf. The green pointed cabbage has leaves that are more open than normal (they have a softer texture and sweeter taste too). Add it to stir-fries or serve it with butter and black pepper as a side.

JANUARY KING (bottom right)
A January King's rich purple is totally dependent on the weather: the more extreme, the deeper the purple. It only needs a gentle steam if you want the purple to reign.

SAVOY (bottom left)
Not to be confused with the hotel, the Savoy's pleasingly nutty flavour and attractive bubble-wrap texture makes it much more interesting to eat than bricks and mortar. It's a versatile cabbage and absolutely brilliant when braised.

SPRING GREENS
These are the fast-and-loose boys of the cabbage world. They have big blousy leaves and their centre cores are not as tight as other varieties. As the name implies, they're typically the first cabbage to arrive in spring.

TUNDRA (top right)
Tundra is like Scott of the Antarctic; it doesn't seem to mind harsh winter weather. Because of its crisp texture, you can cook it any way you like.

Perfect Poached Chicken & Wild Garlic Gremolata Broth

If you're looking for incredibly tender meat and a gorgeous chicken broth, then poaching is your pot of gold. Add a swirl of olive-glossed gremolata (a Milanese mix of lemon, garlic and parsley) and you have a splendidly comforting bowl of wonder.

 20 MINS · 1 HR 50 MINS · 6

2kg whole organic chicken

1 garlic bulb

1 large carrot, scrubbed and halved

1–2 celery sticks, roughly chopped

1 large onion, roughly chopped

A large handful of foraged wild garlic or fresh parsley

1 lemon

2–3 tbsp olive oil

Sea salt and freshly ground pepper

Remove the giblets from inside the chicken. Place the bird in a large pot. Arrange the giblets (all except the chicken liver) in the pot around the chicken to enrich the stock.

Slice your garlic bulb in half horizontally (set aside two halved cloves for later). Place the garlic, carrot, celery and onion in and around the bird.

Season. Fully cover the bird with water, or as close to the top as possible. Bring to the boil. Turn the heat right down. Cover. Simmer for 1½ hrs.

Before the end of the poaching time, preheat your oven to 200°C/ Gas 6. Uncover the pot and transfer it to your heated oven. Roast for 20 mins or till golden on top.

Remove the chicken from the pot. The legs should come away when gently tugged. If not, roast for a little longer.

Strain the veg and giblets from the broth. Bring the broth to a gentle simmer. Finely chop the wild garlic or parsley, the zest from your lemon and the reserved garlic cloves. Mix in a bowl with the olive oil (enough to make a loose, pesto-like sauce) and some salt and pepper.

Thinly slice your lemon. Flick out the pips. Add the lemon slices to the simmering broth along with a good swirl of the gremolata.

Shred or slice the chicken and serve with the herby broth. Delicious served in shallow bowls with pots of extra gremolata on the side.

Asparagus & Egg-Fried Quinoa

Did someone say brunch? Wake up (very slowly indeed) to this twist on traditional egg-fried rice, with quinoa and seasonal asparagus. This one tastes even better if you stay in your pyjamas.

 **V** 🥄15 MINS 🍲20 MINS 🍴4 ♡2

150g quinoa

400g asparagus

1 chilli

4 eggs

2 tbsp oil (any kind – coconut oil is nice here)

3cm ginger, grated

2 garlic cloves, grated

A bunch of spring onions, thinly sliced

2 tbsp tamari

1 lime, zest and juice

A large handful of chervil, chives and/or sorrel, chopped

Sea salt and freshly ground pepper

Rinse your quinoa till the water runs clear. Set a small lidded pan over a high heat. Add the quinoa and a pinch of salt. Pour in enough water to cover the quinoa by 1cm (about 300ml). Cover and simmer for 15 mins or till all the water is absorbed.

Turn the heat off. Keep the quinoa covered for 5 mins.

Cut your asparagus into 3–4cm chunks. Cut a few thin slices from your chilli, more or less, to taste. Crack your eggs into a bowl and whisk.

Once the quinoa is done, set a wok or large frying pan over a high heat. Add the oil. Fold in the chilli, ginger and garlic. Sizzle for 1 min.

Add the asparagus and cook till just tender. Tip the spring onions in. Stir-fry for 1 min. Add the quinoa. Fry everything for 1 min. Add the tamari.

Push everything to one side in the pan, giving you space to add your eggs. Add a little more oil if the pan's looking dry. Add the eggs. Once set, fold the egg through the mix, breaking it up as you fold.

Finish your quinoa with a little lime zest, a good squeeze of lime juice and a handful of chopped herbs. Season with salt and pepper to taste.

Asparagus Benedict Royale

Rise, shine, wonder where your slippers are then dish up flaky Jersey Royals, seasonal asparagus and organic eggs for breakfast. This is our royal take on classic eggs Benedict.

 V   10 MINS   35 MINS   2   1

500g Jersey Royal or new potatoes

1 tbsp olive oil

A bundle of asparagus

1 garlic clove, finely chopped

1 lemon, zest and juice

4 duck eggs, plus 2 yolks

A pinch of saffron (optional)

45g butter

A handful of chervil, sorrel or chives

Sea salt and freshly ground pepper

Preheat your oven to 200°C/Gas 6. Place a large roasting tin on the top shelf of your oven to heat up.

Give your potatoes a good scrub. Cut into 0.5-1cm slices. Toss into the warmed roasting tin. Drizzle with the olive oil. Season. Give them a shake to coat the potatoes in the seasoned oil. Roast for 25 mins or till golden.

Meanwhile, snap the woody ends from your asparagus.

When the potatoes are golden, stir the garlic and lemon zest through them. Pile the asparagus on top. Put back in the oven for 5 mins or till the asparagus is just tender.

Place your egg yolks in a large bowl with 1 tbsp of the lemon juice and the saffron, if using. Season. Melt your butter in a pan. As soon as it's melted, gradually pour the butter into your egg yolks, whisking constantly till you have a creamy sauce. Spoon the sauce into the butter pan. Set aside.

Fill a small pan with boiling water. Bring back to the boil.

Crack one egg into a small dish. Gently slide the egg into the water. Pop the lid on. Cook till the white is set and the yolk is as firm or soft as you like it. Remove with a slotted spoon and pop the egg in a bowl. Repeat with the rest of the eggs.

Finely chop your herbs, saving a few sprigs for later. Mix the chopped herbs through the potato/asparagus mix, along with a drizzle of lemon juice. Pile onto plates. Top with your poached eggs. Gently warm the butter sauce and spoon over the top. Garnish with the saved herbs and a pinch of pepper.

Crispy Buckwheat with Saffron Yogurt & Asparagus

The season for British asparagus is all too brief, so make hay while the sun shines, say we. Here, the thick spears are generously drizzled with rich, tangy saffron yogurt for a weekday (or any day) treat.

 V · 5 MINS · 20 MINS · 2 · 2½

150g buckwheat

350ml veg stock

250g cherry vine tomatoes

3 tbsp olive oil

1 tsp cumin seeds

250g asparagus

150g Greek-style yogurt

A pinch of saffron powder

1 lemon

Sea salt and freshly ground pepper

Preheat your oven to 180°C/Gas 4. Tip the buckwheat into a pan and cover with the stock. Simmer for 15 mins till tender, then drain.

While the buckwheat cooks, arrange the cherry tomatoes on a baking tray. Toss with 1 tbsp of the olive oil and a sprinkle of salt and pepper. Roast in the hot oven for 15 mins.

Heat a large dry frying pan over a medium heat for 1 min. Sprinkle in the cumin seeds and toast for 2–3 minutes, then tip into a bowl.

When the buckwheat is cooked, pour 2 tbsp of the oil into the frying pan you used to toast the cumin seeds. Add the buckwheat. Fry for 5 mins, stirring frequently, till crispy. Stir in most of the toasted cumin seeds and season well.

Trim the asparagus. Add to the roasting tray with the tomatoes after 15 mins. Roast for a further 5 mins.

Spoon the yogurt into a bowl and fold in the saffron powder, the juice from half the lemon and a little salt and pepper. Cut the remaining lemon half into wedges.

Heap the buckwheat onto each plate. Arrange the asparagus and cherry tomatoes on top. Scatter over the remaining toasted cumin seeds and serve with dollops of the saffron yogurt and lemon wedges.

Magic Miso & Sesame Dressing

Ah, the mysterious umami – the fifth taste that joins sweet, sour, bitter and salt. Miso is the poster child for umami and absolutely loves asparagus. Mind, it'll just as easily cosy up to grilled aubergine slices or cherry tomatoes before you roast them.

 15 MINS 3-5 MINS 2 1

250g asparagus

½ tbsp brown rice miso

1 tbsp sesame oil

2 tbsp water

1cm ginger, grated

2 tbsp sesame seeds

1 spring onion, thinly sliced on the diagonal

Fire up your barbecue or get a griddle pan at the ready.

Snap the woody ends off your asparagus. Whisk the miso, sesame oil, water and ginger together. Whisk to a smooth paste.

Set a small frying pan over a medium heat. Add your sesame seeds. Toast till just golden.

Place the asparagus on the barbecue (or a smoking hot griddle pan). Cook for 3-5 mins, turning now and then, till charred.

Lift the charred spears onto a serving dish. Drizzle with the miso dressing. Scatter with the toasted sesame seeds. Garnish with the sliced spring onion.

Unhomogenised Milk

In the 1930s, a process was invented to break apart fat molecules under high pressure, leaving the fat suspended and evenly dispersed throughout the milk. Some folks thought it made the milk look better. However, we love a creamy cap on the top of our milk and find it easier to digest that way. We also adore our dairy king and queen, Nick and Christine Gosling. They have supplied Abel & Cole with milk for donkeys.

Salt & Butter-Cracked Radishes

Bold, crunchy and with a peppery bite, radishes are simply ravishing. Fold through a batch of freshly cooked or leftover quinoa for a speedy lunch or try with a sprinkle of pistachios and a dollop of Greek yogurt.

(V) 🔪 10 MINS 🍳 5 MINS 🍴 2-4 ❤ 1-2

A bunch of radishes

A knob of butter

A few radish leaves

A handful of fresh mint leaves, finely chopped

Sea salt

Trim and wash your radishes, reserving the leaves. Use the end of a rolling pin or blunt object to bash each radish so it just opens up slightly (hence: cracked).

Set a frying pan over a high heat. Add the butter. Let it just melt. Chuck the radishes in the pan. Toss through the melted butter.

Take off the heat. Add a pinch of salt and the mint leaves.

TOTALLY RADISHING

Spring Up Salmon Caesar

Rich in Omega 3, salmon and avocado (full of the good kind of fat) will really get the motor running first thing in the morning (or any time of day for that matter). Erm, speaking figuratively, of course. You'll probably still need keys to start your motor.

20 MINS, PLUS OVERNIGHT SOAKING (IF POSSIBLE)　　0 (OR 5 MINS)　　2-4　　2-3

For the dressing:

50g cashews

4 anchovies or 1 tbsp capers

1 lemon, zest and 3 tbsp juice

1 tbsp Dijon mustard

2 tsp Worcestershire sauce

1 small garlic clove

125ml olive oil

Sea salt and freshly ground pepper

For the salad:

A bunch of radishes

1 avocado

100g lamb's lettuce or peppery salad mix

1 fennel bulb, halved and thinly sliced

A large handful of chervil, dill and/or sorrel, roughly chopped

120g organic smoky roast salmon, flaked

Soak your cashews in a jar full of water overnight. If you don't have time, simmer in enough water to cover for 5 mins or till softened. Drain. Rinse.

Pop the soaked cashews in a food processor or blender with all the other dressing ingredients apart from the olive oil. Blend to make a smooth paste. Keep blending as you trickle the oil in, little by little. Season to taste. Chill till ready to use. Blend in a little water, if needed, to thin the dressing to single-cream consistency.

Pluck any wilted leaves from your radishes. Thinly slice your radishes and roughly chop the nice-looking leaves (compost the wilted ones). Halve your avocado, remove the stone, peel and cut into slices (or plonk the halves in the salad, unsliced, as we did).

Toss all the salad leaves, prepped veg and herbs together. Arrange in bowls. Dot the flaked salmon over the top. Drizzle with the dressing before serving.

Sweet & Sour Rhubarb Pork with Egg-Fried Rice

Fancy a takeaway? This one's prepped in less time than it'll take you to find a suitable app. Tonight it's egg-fried rice with two spring co-stars – rhubarb and pork.

 15 MINS 30 MINS 4 1

200g brown basmati rice

400ml boiling water

4 eggs

100g breadcrumbs

4 pork escalopes

6 rhubarb sticks

3cm ginger, grated

2 oranges, zest and juice

100ml water

1 tbsp Demerara sugar

1 tbsp olive oil

6 spring onions, thinly sliced

A handful of flat leaf parsley, roughly chopped

Sea salt and freshly ground pepper

Preheat your oven to 180°C/Gas 4. Tip the rice into a small pan. Pour in the boiling water. Cover. Simmer over a very low heat for 20–25 mins till all the water has been absorbed. Take off the heat. Leave to steam, lid on, for 5 mins.

Line a baking tray with baking paper. Crack 1 egg into a bowl. Season and whisk. Spread the breadcrumbs on a large plate. Slice the pork escalopes into strips as big as your little finger. Dip the pork strips into the egg. Roll in the breadcrumbs, making sure they are well coated. Lay on the baking tray.

Bake the pork strips in the oven for 15 mins. (Turn them over halfway through.)

Meanwhile, trim and slice the rhubarb into 1cm chunks.

Put half the rhubarb into a pan with the ginger and a little zest and all the juice from your oranges. Add the water. Cook for 5 mins till the rhubarb has softened into a puree.

Add the remaining rhubarb to the orangey/rhubarb puree. Add the sugar. Cook for 2 mins till the second batch of rhubarb is a little soft.

Beat the remaining 3 eggs in a bowl with a pinch of salt. Heat a frying pan with the oil. Fry the spring onions for 1 min. Pour in the eggs and cook for 2 mins till set. With a wooden spoon, break up the egg.

Tip in the cooked rice. Cook for 2 mins till the rice is coated in the egg and piping hot. Add the parsley. Serve with the crispy pork strips and rhubarb sweet and sour sauce.

Sugar & Spice
Most of rhubarb's fructose is stored in its white ends. Don't chop them off entirely. Just trim the brown bits and you'll get a sweeter sauce.

Grilled PSB Satay

This sublime satay dressing is superb with our seasonal favourite, purple sprouting broccoli. It can also be quickly whipped up and served with just about any veg you can think of: roasted squash, griddled aubergine, courgettes, or use it as a dip for raw veg (carrots, celery and more...).

 10 MINS 10 MINS 4 1

350-400g purple sprouting broccoli

A drizzle of olive or sesame oil

3 tbsp peanut butter

1 tbsp soy sauce

1 garlic clove

3cm ginger

A pinch of chilli powder (optional)

1 lime, cut into wedges

1 tbsp rice or cider vinegar

1 tbsp honey or maple syrup

1 tsp ground turmeric or 2cm fresh turmeric, peeled

3 tbsp water

A handful of coriander, chervil or parsley, to serve (optional)

Sea salt

Set your oven grill to high (or fire up the barbecue).

Trim the woody ends from your broccoli. Halve or quarter any larger/thicker pieces so they're roughly all the same size.

Flash your broccoli under or on the grill in a single layer. Drizzle and dust with a little oil and salt. Cook, turning once or twice, till tender and lightly charred around the edges, about 10 mins.

In a food processor, blend the peanut butter, soy sauce, garlic, ginger, chilli, 1 tbsp of lime juice from the wedges, vinegar, honey/maple syrup and turmeric to make a smooth paste. Taste. Add a little more of anything you fancy to make it just right for you. Thin with up to 3 tablespooons of water, if needed, to reach the consistency of double cream.

Use as a dip, or drizzle or dollop the sauce over the grilled broccoli. Lovely served with wedges of lime and a sprinkling of finely chopped herbs.

Korean Kiwi Dressing

This dressing is like Romeo to Julienne. A zinger of a dressing that's brilliant tossed in a cold noodle salad with plenty of julienne veg. A star-crossed pairing if ever there was one – only with less tragedy.

 5 MINS 0 2-4 ½-1

2 ripe kiwis

½ tsp freshly grated ginger

½ tsp tamari

2 tbsp cold water

2 tbsp olive or sesame oil

A few slices of fresh chilli

1 lime, zest and a squeeze of juice

Honey or agave syrup (optional)

Sea salt

Halve your kiwis. Scoop the flesh into a blender or food processor. Add the rest of the ingredients and a pinch of salt. Blend till smooth. Taste. Tweak the flavours till you're happy. If your kiwi aren't quite ripe or sweet enough, add a little honey or agave syrup.

Rhuby, Thyme, Lime & Almond Tart

Rhubarb, rhubarb, rhubarb; we could wax lyrical about this ingredient all day long. A poster child of spring, and don't get us started on the fruit-or-veg debate. This beautiful, striped tart makes bold use of its colour with some added zing courtesy of lime and fresh thyme.

V · 30 MINS + AT LEAST 60 MINS' CHILLING/RESTING · 60 MINS · 8 · ½

For the pastry:
125g butter

250g sprouted spelt flour (or wholemeal)

50g icing sugar

1 egg yolk

Ice-cold water

For the filling:
225g ground almonds

200g butter

175g golden caster sugar

2 eggs

2 tbsp plain flour

1 tsp baking powder

1 lime, zest and juice

A handful of picked thyme leaves

6–8 rhubarb sticks

For the topping:
1 lime, zest and juice

1 tbsp honey

1 tbsp water

A handful of thyme leaves, to serve

Coarsely grate the butter for the pastry into a large bowl. Sift in the spelt flour and the icing sugar. Rub together with your fingertips to form fine breadcrumbs.

Pour in the egg yolk and stir through with a fork. Trickle in a little cold water to form a dough. Lightly bring together, taking care not to overwork.

Wrap the dough in cling film and pop into the fridge for at least 30 mins.

Roll the dough out on a lightly floured surface into a large circle. Line your 24cm tart tin with the pastry. Pop into the fridge to chill for 30 mins. Spelt flour tends to result in a slightly crumblier pastry, so patch any holes or cracks.

Preheat your oven to 180°C/Gas 4.

Remove the pastry case from the fridge and cover with a large sheet of baking paper. Fill with baking beans, rice or coins. Blind-bake in the preheated oven for 20 mins. Lift out the baking paper and beans and slide back into the oven for 10 mins.

While your pastry case is cooking, beat together the filling ingredients (except the rhubarb). It should be light and creamy. Pop into the fridge.

Once the pastry has cooked for the final 10 mins, trim any rough or overhanging edges.

Spoon in the almond filling. Use a spatula to spread it to the edges and to smooth the surface.

Arrange the rhubarb over the top, trimming to fit the tin, if needed. Slide into the oven to cook for 25–30 mins, till the almond filling is set and golden.

While the tart is cooking, heat the lime juice, honey and water in a pan. Bring to a bubble, then take off the heat. When the tart has cooked, generously brush this glaze over the top.

Garnish with the lime zest and a few thyme leaves.

Bananas About Macaroons

Just a handful of ingredients and not a jot of sugar. These are a winner and a handy treat to have up your sleeve for big or small hands who need something sweet at the drop of a hat. (We do not recommend storing macaroons up your sleeve.)

 V · 10 MINS · 10–12 MINS · 20

2 bananas, peeled

125g desiccated coconut

Seeds from ½ vanilla pod or ½ tsp vanilla extract

1 egg

Sea salt

Preheat your oven to 180°C/Gas 4. Line a baking sheet with baking paper.

Put the bananas, coconut and vanilla into a bowl with a pinch of salt.

Mush it all up and give it a squidgy mix with your hands or with a large spoon or fork.

Crack the egg in. Mix it well.

Scoop out a rounded teaspoonful. Roll into a little ball in your hands. Pop on the lined baking sheet. Repeat until you have used up all the mixture.

Press each cookie flat with the back of a fork. Bake for 10–12 mins or till a little golden around the edges.

Delicious on their own, or you can finish them off with a drizzling of melted chocolate.

Kiwi Sorbet

Looking to chill out with some sorbet? Your own fruit bowl's better than any tub. Make this with from scratch and we promise it'll dish out more healthy and exciting flavours than you can shake a banana at.

 5 MINS   FREEZING TIME: OVERNIGHT OR AT LEAST 4 HRS   2   1

4 kiwi fruit

1 tbsp icing sugar (more or less, to taste)

A pinch of ground cinnamon

Peel and dice your kiwi and put in a freezer-proof container. Freeze till fully firm.

Toss the frozen kiwi in a food processor or blender with the icing sugar and cinnamon. Blend till smooth. Add more sugar, if needed. Serve straight away.

Golden Milkshake

A dairy-free milkshake with the Midas touch. You've struck gold with this one. Five mins to make and down the hatch in even less we bet – it's just that good.

 5 MINS 0 4 1

400ml coconut milk or kefir

4 bananas

5cm fresh turmeric

A little ice and/or water

Tip the coconut milk or kefir into a blender. Peel your bananas and turmeric. Add to the blender. Whizz till smooth. Add a little water to thin and/or ice to chill, as you like.

Freeze!
For a richer, creamier milkshake, peel, roughly chop and freeze your bananas first.

Smoothie in a Jar'O

Miles better for you than a jar of whiskey (or a pint of Guinness). Fire up your blender and bring together spring's bounty in one glass. It is easy being green after all.

 5 MINS 0 2 2½

1 ripe avocado

2 bananas

100g baby leaf spinach

1 lime, zest and juice

A handful of mint, leaves only

250ml water

Halve and stone the avocado. Scoop the flesh into a blender or food processor. Add the peeled bananas, spinach, lime zest and juice, and mint leaves. Trickle in the water and blend till smooth. Add more water if needed.

Rhuby G&T

There's something quintessentially British about a good gin and tonic and this one's even more spiffing, thanks to some seasonal rhubarb.

 5 MINS, PLUS 2-3 DAYS FOR INFUSING   0   ABOUT A DOZEN G&TS

3-4 rhubarb sticks

½ vanilla pod

750ml gin (see tip)

2 tbsp honey or agave syrup (more or less, to taste)

Tonic water, to serve

Set aside ¼ of a stick of rhubarb for garnishing if you like. Thinly slice the rest and pack into a 1-litre jar (or a few smaller ones). Slip in the vanilla pod and add the gin. Swirl in the honey or agave syrup. Shake, taste and add more sweetener if you think it needs it.

Store in a cool dark place for at least 2-3 days or till it's infused to your desired potency, up to 2-3 weeks.

Strain the rhubarb and vanilla out. Pour the gin into ice-packed tumblers with curls of rhubarb (made using a veg peeler) and top up with tonic. Or for a really fancy cocktail, Prosecco.

Teetotal? No probs.

Juice the rhubarb and simmer with the vanilla and honey to make a syrup base for a virgin cocktail. Delicious with tonic or sparkling elderflower.

Or you can infuse the rhubarb with vanilla and honey in 350ml of cider vinegar to make a shrub. Store at room temperature or in the fridge, and strain once the vinegar has lapped up enough rhubarb flavour (2-3 weeks). Serve with sparkling water or sparkling elderflower.

Carroty Carrot Cookies

Look, if it looks like a carrot it's good for you, isn't it? These even have some veg in them. Treats are okay now and then, so these spiced cookies are just the ticket for Easter. Hop about the kitchen (safely) while you whip these up.

 (V) 20 MINS, PLUS 2 HRS' CHILLING   15 MINS   18-20   ¼

For the cookies:

110g butter, softened

200g caster sugar

1 egg

½ tsp vanilla extract or seeds from 1 vanilla pod

250g plain flour, plus extra for dusting

40g oats

1 tsp baking powder

1 tsp mixed spice

¼ tsp ground ginger

150g carrots, finely grated

50g walnuts, finely chopped

50g raisins

1 orange, zest

Sea salt

For the icing (optional):

300g icing sugar

1 orange, juice

Orange food colouring (optional)

To decorate (optional):

Thyme or rosemary sprigs

Cream the butter and sugar together till light and fluffy. Beat the egg and vanilla together, add to the creamed butter and sugar, and mix well. Add the rest of the ingredients and a pinch of salt, and stir together till well combined.

Put the cookie mix into the fridge and leave to chill for at least 2 hrs.

Preheat your oven to 180°C/Gas 4.

Remove the dough from the fridge. Dust your work surface liberally with flour. Place half the dough onto the floured surface. Dust a little more flour over the top. Pat it down using your hands into a large circle. It should be about 0.5cm thick. Don't worry, the dough will be a little sticky.

Using a sharp knife, cut out thin triangles approximately 7cm long. Or use a carrot-shaped cookie cutter if you have one. Repeat with the other half of the dough.

Place on a lined baking tray or two, 2cm apart as they will spread during cooking. Slide into the oven and bake for 15 mins till golden.

Remove the cookies from the oven and leave to cool slightly. Lift them on to a cooling rack. Leave to cool completely.

While the cookies are cooling, tip the icing sugar into a bowl. Squeeze in the juice from ½ orange and mix. The icing should form peaks when you lift the spoon from the bowl. Add more orange juice or icing sugar as needed. Add the orange food colouring, if using.

When the cookies have cooled, pipe or spread the icing on to the cookies. Gently push a sprig of thyme or rosemary into the top of each cookie to represent carrot leaves.

Jolly Beans

We're bonkers about organic chocolate. Cocoa pods are often very heavily sprayed and it's good to know you're not imbibing a cocktail of chemicals when you reach for a square of the good stuff.

And the feel-good factor doesn't end there. Organic farming means there are no chemical run-offs into local waterways, which is especially important in countries where water isn't always on tap.

A principle of organic farming is to be a positive part of the local community, and protecting the health of the human beans who live nearby.

White Choc Passion Puds

You've hit the jackpot on the passionfruit machine. This is a simple and stunning white choc truffle pot filled with molten, fresh passionfruit toffee. We weren't kidding. Enjoy your winnings.

 V · 10 MINS · 10 MINS · 4 · ½

100g white chocolate

75ml double or luxury pouring cream

6 passionfruit

About 75g caster sugar or 35g honey

Put the white chocolate and cream in a heatproof bowl that sits snugly over a saucepan or another bowl. Fill the saucepan or larger bowl with a shallow pool of boiling water. Set the chocolate bowl on top.

Once you can see the chocolate melting, gently stir till the mix is silky smooth. Add more boiling water to your supporting pan/bowl if needed.

Divide your chocolate mix between little tea cups or ramekins and leave to cool. Pop in the freezer to set for 30 mins.

Set a fine mesh sieve over a pan or bowl. Halve your passionfruit. Scoop the seeds into the sieve. Squeeze them and press with the back of a large spoon to get out as much juice as possible.

Measure the juice: you should have around 150ml. Add the same weight of sugar (or half the weight of honey) to the juice. Bring to the boil. Be careful not to let it bubble over. Reduce the heat to a gentle, rolling boil. Cook for 5 mins, or till it's thickened into a nice, egg-yolky (in colour and consistency) syrup. Remove from the heat.

Once your truffle pots are set, dip a small spoon into a mug of boiling water. Scoop a little circle from the centre of each pot. Save for another time (or eat!). When all your pots have their centres removed, gently reheat your passionfruit syrup. Add a drop of water to loosen a little, if needed (though try to keep the consistency thick). Pour the syrup into the centres of the puds. Serve.

Quick Pickled Rhubarb

Whisk 4 tbsp of red wine vinegar with 2 tbsp of caster sugar or honey, 1 tsp of finely grated ginger and a pinch of cinnamon. Trim a stalk of rhubarb into 5cm lengths. Run a veg peeler down the lengths to make fine ribbons. Fold the rhubarb through the vinegar. Pile into a sterilised jam jar (see page 114). Steep in the fridge for at least 30 mins or up to 1 week. Delicious with roast pork or fried rice.

Banana & Peanut Butter Mousse

Blend a ripe banana with 1 tbsp of peanut butter (or any nut butter). Add a little cinnamon, vanilla and/or nutmeg, if you like. Dust the top with cocoa powder if you fancy your mousse cappuccino-style.

Carrot-Top Seaweed

Wash your green carrot tops really well. Pat dry. Finely chop. Massage in a pinch of salt, a pinch of sugar and a gloss of olive or coconut oil. Fry in a large pan, adding more oil if needed, till crisp like Chinese seaweed.

Radish Top & Walnut Pesto

Thoroughly wash your green radish tops. Whizz with a large handful of toasted walnuts, a small garlic clove and a few nuggets of a hard goats' cheese. Add some fresh basil or tarragon, too, if you've got it. Trickle in enough olive oil to bring it together. Toss with puy lentils and thinly sliced radishes.

Caraway Cabbage Noodles

Finely shred a green cabbage or head of spring greens. Pile into a pot of salted, boiling water. Cook till just tender, 1–2 mins. Drain. Toast some caraway seeds (or cumin seeds). Add a lump of butter (or olive oil) and a pinch of salt. Fold through the shredded cabbage. Delicious as a Sunday roast side.

Asparagus & Mint Pesto

Blitz 2 handfuls of roughly chopped asparagus (you can use the woody ends for this, too – or just the woody ends) with a handful of toasted cashews or pine nuts, a small garlic clove and a large handful of fresh mint leaves. Add enough olive oil (or you could whip in butter, making it more like a pâté) to bring to a paste. Thin with a little lime juice and/or water. Gorgeous as a dip or tossed with boiled Jersey Royals.

SUMMER

Long days and lazy brunches are in.
Mindfully pod broad beans, forage for elderflower,
swoon over naturally sweet strawberries, tomatoes and
stone fruit. Throw a sustainable mackerel
on the barbie and jump for joy.

·····················

Seasonal Stars

Broad beans, lettuce, new potatoes,
tomatoes, courgettes, melon, nectarines, strawberries,
aubergines, elderflower.

·····················

Wonderful One-Pot Summer Spaghetti

Beans, beans, the musical fruit... The more you eat, the more you support seasonal British farmers. Pay no heed to the length of this one. It's an easy and fantastic way to celebrate summer veg without loads of washing up.

(V) (🕐) 15 MINS (🍳) 15 MINS (🍴) 2 (❤) 3 (4 IF YOU SERVE WITH COURGETTI)

1 lemon

25g pine nuts

500g broad beans

3 tbsp olive oil

½ tsp salt

1 garlic clove, thinly sliced

250g cherry vine tomatoes, quartered

200g spaghetti (or courgetti, see page 94)

1 spring onion, finely sliced

A large handful of basil, leaves only

50g watercress or pea shoots

Freshly ground pepper

Finely grate the zest from the lemon and juice one half (keep the other half for later).

Heat a large, heavy-based pan for 2 mins. Tip in the pine nuts and toast for 2–3 mins till golden. Tip out into a bowl. Fill the pan with water and bring to a boil.

While the water is coming to the boil, pop the broad beans from their pods. When the water is bubbling, drop in the beans. Cook for 2 mins. Drain into a jug and reserve 500ml of the cooking water. Plunge the beans into ice-cold water to stop them cooking further.

Pour the reserved cooking water back into the pan and bring back to the boil. Add the oil, salt, garlic, lemon zest, lemon juice and cherry tomatoes.

Snap the spaghetti in half and add it to the pan (see tip if you're going for courgetti instead). Clamp on a lid till the water comes back to the boil again. Remove the lid. Simmer on a high heat for 8 mins. Toss the pasta every now and then while it cooks.

Meanwhile, pop the broad beans out of their grey skins. The easiest way to do this is to pinch one end and squeeze so they pop out. This is optional: when broad beans are young like this the grey skins aren't too tough. But they will look greener without their skins.

After 8 mins, the spaghetti should be al dente (soft with a slight bite) and most of the water evaporated. Throw in the broad beans and the spring onion. Toss together for 1 min to warm through.

Add most of the basil and fold it through the spaghetti with a crack of pepper. Add more salt if needed. Tangle into warm bowls, spooning over any sauce and the veg. Top with the remaining basil, the watercress or pea shoots and toasted pine nuts. Cut the remaining half lemon into wedges, and serve on the side.

Spag Swaps

You can use any pasta, just cook it as long as it says on the packet. For courgetti, you can either have it raw or boil it for 1 min just to soften it. Season well, gloss with olive oil and carry on as above.

Whipped Minted Broad Beans

For nights or days when you want to soak up every last bit of summer sun – you can leave your pods on (sung to the tune of 'Leave Your Hat On'). With hardly any effort, you can make this cracker of a recipe. Excellent with new season lamb, too. Result!

 V 15 MINS 2-3 MINS 4 1

1 kg fresh broad beans in their pods (or 350g shelled broad beans or peas)

1 garlic clove

200g feta or a soft, creamy ewes' cheese

20g fresh mint leaves, plus extra to serve

1 lemon, zest and juice

A pinch of chilli powder or fresh chilli

2 tbsp olive oil

Sea salt and freshly ground pepper

Shell the beans and blanch for 2-3 minutes until tender. Run under cold water, then pop the inner beans out of their grey skins by making a small tear and gently squeezing them out.

Place the beans, garlic, feta, mint leaves, lemon zest and juice, and olive oil into a food processor, with a pinch of chilli and pepper. Blitz till as smooth or chunky as you like it. No food processor? Just mash everything up with a potato masher, fork or in a pestle and mortar. Adjust seasoning to taste.

Spoon out onto a serving plate and drizzle with olive oil. Scatter a few small mint leaves over the top. Serve with crudites or garlic-rubbed slices of toasted and olive oil-glossed sourdough.

Dairy-free?

Swap the feta and olive oil for 150ml coconut milk or coconut yogurt and a pinch of salt. Add more coconut milk or yogurt, if needed, until you get a houmous-like consistency.

Popping Summer Bean Energy Salad

They say it takes two to tango and this pop-ish dressing dances moreishly with the ace duo of beans and peas.

(V) 🥄 20 MINS 🍲 5 MINS 🍴 4 ♥ 1

500g broad beans

200g sugar snap peas

1 red onion, finely chopped

1 garlic clove, crushed

1 tbsp honey

2 tbsp brown rice vinegar

2 tsp black onion seeds

3 tbsp olive oil

2 tsp black mustard seeds

1 tsp coriander seeds

1 red chilli, thinly sliced

A handful of tarragon, leaves only

Sea salt and freshly ground pepper

Pop the broad beans out of their pods. Drop into a pan of boiling water. Simmer for 2 mins. Lift them out with a slotted spoon and plunge into ice water. Drop the sugar snap peas into the boiling water (keep them whole as you can eat the pods). Cook for 1 min. Drain. Plunge them into a separate bowl of iced water.

Pop the onion and garlic into a jam jar. Add the honey, vinegar, black onion seeds and 1 tbsp of the olive oil. Season. Screw on the lid and shake.

Pop the broad beans out of their grey skins. Drain the sugar snap peas and pat dry with kitchen towel. Lay on a large serving platter. Scatter the broad beans over the top.

Heat a frying pan on a medium heat. When hot, pour in 2 tbsp of the oil. Tip in the mustard seeds and coriander seeds. Fry them for about 2 mins till they pop. Remove from the heat and stir in the chilli.

Toss the beans and peas through the pink onion dressing. Spoon the popping hot oil over the top. Scatter with the tarragon leaves.

Food in the Nude

There's nothing better than a freshly harvested summer lettuce. We love all the amazing varieties that come in from the fields over summer. Most of all though, we love the lack of chemical residues.

Leafy lettuces like these have a very large surface area, which means a non-organic lettuce can come with free pesticide and insecticide residues. Doesn't sound so delicious, does it? We prefer ours naturally naked.

Lettuce Tartlettes

The number one rule of picnic food? No cutlery! These tartlets are fork-free and portable.

(V) 30 MINS, PLUS 1 HR CHILLING | 35 MINS | 8 LITTLE TARTS | ½ PER TART

150g plain white flour

100g Parmesan (or equivalent), grated

100g cold unsalted butter, cubed, plus a little extra for greasing

4-5 tbsp cold water

150g lettuce (see tip), finely chopped

3-4 spring onions, finely chopped

½ lemon, zest

A handful of tarragon, mint, chives and/or basil leaves, finely chopped

4 egg yolks

200g crème fraîche

2 tsp Dijon mustard

Freshly ground pepper

Mix the flour and half the Parmesan together in a large bowl.

Add the butter and rub it into the flour and cheese with your hands, till it resembles breadcrumbs. Bind it with a trickle of the water. Shape into a smooth ball. Wrap in cling film. Chill for 1 hr in the fridge.

Preheat your oven to 200°C/Gas 6. Brush 6-8 mini tart tins with a little oil or butter. Coarsely grate some of the chilled pastry into each tin. Press evenly into the sides and base. Line with baking paper. Fill with coins or baking beans. Bake for 10 mins, or till just golden. Turn the oven down to 180°C/Gas 4.

In a bowl, mix together the lettuce, spring onions, lemon zest, remaining Parmesan, fresh herbs and lots of black pepper.

Whisk the egg yolks, crème fraîche and mustard together in a bowl. Stir the lettuce mix into the eggy mixture. Spoon into the pastry cases. Bake for 25 mins, or till golden and set.

Take Your Pick

Any lettuce apart from iceberg works. Or try watercress: don't chop the leaves, just the stalks.

Griddled Romaine & Minted Tahini Yogurt Sauce

Always eat lettuce raw? We're fans of that, for sure, but cooking it doubles your options. Here, we griddle it to intensify the flavour. The gorgeous summer dressing is a cracker, too.

V 15 MINS 5 MINS 2 1

1 lemon

2 tbsp tahini

2 tbsp cold water

1 tbsp + 4 tsp olive oil

150g Greek-style yogurt

A handful of mint leaves, finely chopped

2 mini romaine lettuces

A handful of dill leaves

Sea salt and freshly ground pepper

Zest and juice half your lemon into a large bowl. Squeeze in the tahini. Pour in the cold water and 1 tbsp of oil. Whisk together with a pinch of salt till smooth and creamy. Spoon in half the yogurt and swirl it through the tahini dressing.

Finely chop the mint leaves and fold through the tahini yogurt. Taste and season. Add more lemon zest or juice to taste.

Set a griddle or frying pan on a high heat. Cut the mini romaines in half, slicing through the root, to keep the leaves together. Pull off any tatty outer leaves.

Rub 1 tsp of oil onto the cut side of each romaine and sprinkle with salt. Place cut-side down into the hot griddle pan and cook for 5 mins till charred and softened.

Place the charred romaines onto a serving platter. Drizzle with the tahini yogurt. Scatter with the dill leaves.

Chilled-Out Lemon, Lettuce & Avocado Soup

On a hot summer's day, this one's just the ticket to whip up nice and quickly, and get back outside to soak up some rays.

 10 MINS · 0 · 4 · 2

2 ripe avocados

1 large or 2 small lettuces, roughly chopped

30g chives or 4 spring onions, roughly chopped

A large handful of fresh sorrel and/or basil leaves

4-6 mint sprigs, leaves only

½ veg or chicken stock cube

500-750ml cold water

½ lemon or lime, zest and a squeeze of juice

A swirl of crème fraîche, cream, mascarpone or natural yogurt (optional)

Freshly ground pepper

Halve your avocados. Scoop out the flesh. Discard the stones. Add to a food processor with the lettuce, chives or spring onions, fresh herbs, stock cube and a twist of pepper.

Start blending. Slowly trickle the water in till the soup is as thick as you like.

Add the lemon or lime zest. Whip it through. Taste. Adjust the flavours, adding more herbs, pepper, a little more stock cube, a little salt and/or a squeeze of lemon or lime, as needed.

Finish with a swirl of something creamy, if you like. Serve cold.

If taking to a picnic, chill for a good hour first. Pour into a clean flask, twist the lid on tightly and it'll be cool when you arrive.

Gorgeous with garlic croutons.

Caesar Royals

No one can say for sure who invented the Caesar salad, but it had nowt to do the Romans. And this has not a huge amount to do with a classic Caesar salad, but that doesn't matter because it's amazing.

 15 MINS 20 MINS 4

1kg Jersey Royals or new potatoes

6 garlic cloves

3-4 rosemary sprigs, leaves only, finely chopped

400g crème fraîche

6 anchovies

1 lemon, zest and a good squeeze of juice

Sea salt and freshly ground pepper

Preheat your oven to 200°C/Gas 6.

Bring a pot of salted water to the boil. Give your spuds a good wash. Cook in the boiling water till tender, 15-20 mins. Drain. Rinse under cold water to cool.

Place the garlic cloves (still in their papery skins) in a little ramekin. Place in the oven and roast while your spuds cook, or till squeezably tender.

Strip the garlic skins off. Place the rosemary, garlic, crème fraîche, anchovies, lemon zest and juice in a blender or food processor. Blitz till smooth. No food processor? Just mash and whisk everything together into a bowl till smooth. Add a good hit of pepper and a little salt, if needed.

Serve the Caesar dressing with the spuds for dipping.

Chipped New Potatoes

Look, as far as we're concerned, all potatoes are potential chips. These are wee and a doddle to make so skip the chippy and make them at home.

 10 MINS · 20 MINS · 4

600g new potatoes
2 tbsp olive or rapeseed oil
2 rosemary sprigs, leaves only
2 tbsp cider vinegar
Sea salt

Put a large pan of water on to boil. Scrub the potatoes and chop them into small, bite-size chunks. Add them to the pan of boiling water. Simmer for 5 mins.

Drain the potatoes and shake them in a colander to rough up the edges.

Warm a deep frying pan or wok over a medium heat. Add the oil and the potatoes. Fry for 15 mins, stirring now and then, till golden brown.

While the potatoes fry, finely chop the rosemary leaves. Add them to the potatoes with a pinch of salt and the vinegar. Toss a few times to coat. Serve straight away.

Green & Gold Potato Salad

Give your run-of-the-mill potato salad a sprinkling of gold dust (turmeric and curry powder) and be transported to an exotic country. (Handy if you're staycationing this year.)

(V) **(🌶)** 15 MINS **(🍲)** 20 MINS **(🍴)** 2 AS MAIN (PAIR WITH A SALAD) OR 4 AS A SIDE **(♡)** ½ AS A SIDE, 1 AS A MAIN

1 red onion, thinly sliced

500g new potatoes

1 tbsp olive oil

4 shallots, thinly sliced

200g French beans

150g Greek-style or natural yogurt

1 tsp ground turmeric

1 tsp mild curry powder

1 lemon

Sea salt and freshly ground pepper

Put a large pan of salted water on to boil. Boil the kettle.

Pop the red onion in a bowl and pour in enough boiling water from the kettle to cover it. Set aside to soak.

Scrub the new potatoes and chop them into equal-sized chunks, around 2–3cm across. When the water is boiling, add the potatoes and simmer for 12 mins.

While the potatoes cook, warm a frying pan for 1 min. Add the olive oil and the shallots. Keep the heat low and fry for 5–8 mins till golden and crisp. Lift out of the pan with a slotted spoon and pop on a plate lined with kitchen towel to drain.

While the shallots fry, trim the French beans. When the potatoes have simmered for 12 mins, add the French beans to the pan. Simmer, without the lid on, for 3 mins till the potatoes are cooked through and tender.

Drain the potatoes and French beans. Leave them to steam dry in the colander.

Tip the yogurt into a large bowl. Add the turmeric and curry powder. Finely grate in the lemon zest. Squeeze in the juice from half the lemon. Add a good pinch of salt and pepper and stir together to make the dressing.

Tip the potatoes and beans into the bowl with the yogurt dressing. Drain the red onions and add them too. Toss together so everything is well coated. Heap up into bowls and top with the crisp shallots to serve.

Charred French Beans with Peanut & Tahini Dressing

Grill, crackle and pop is the name of the game for French beans. It gives them a brilliant texture and this sweet-salty, nutty dressing is the icing on the cake. Or, more accurately, the dressing on the beans.

 10 MINS · 10-15 MINS · 4 · 1

400g French beans
1 tbsp olive oil
1 garlic clove, crushed
3 tbsp water
2 tbsp peanut butter
1 tbsp tahini
2 tbsp tamari
½ tbsp cider vinegar
½ tbsp toasted sesame oil
A pinch of dried chilli flakes
Sea salt

Heat your grill to high. Trim the woody ends off the beans. Toss them with the olive oil and a small pinch of sea salt. Spread the beans out on a baking tray. Grill for 10-15 mins till they're a little charred.

While the beans grill, pop the garlic in a small pan. Add the water, peanut butter, tahini, tamari, cider vinegar and toasted sesame oil. Stir together over a low heat for 2–3 mins to warm through.

Place the beans in a serving bowl. Drizzle with the peanut sauce and sprinkle with a pinch of dried chilli flakes.

Hook, Line & Season

From the wild beauty of the Cornish coast to the sandy shores of Norfolk, we're crazy about the British seaside.

Like fruit and veg, fish are affected by the seasons, and not all make for a good catch.

For many breeds, fishing is most sustainable in the late summer and late autumn. They've already reproduced, which helps to protect future populations. They're fit and full of omega-rich oils and minerals like selenium, taurine and zinc. And they taste better when they're not reproducing, too.

We only use fish that's rated 1–3 by the bobbing bods at the Marine Conservation Society. If you're going to eat fish, choose wisely and enjoy the fruits of the sea considerately.

Hake Burgers with Roast Garlic Mayo

Oh, we do like to be beside the seaside... But even if you're not, these burgers will bring the coast to you. Best enjoyed with a side of fresh air.

 20 MINS   45 MINS   4

1 garlic bulb

60g bread

2 tbsp plain flour

1 egg

2 hake fillets

A handful of flat leaf parsley, leaves only, roughly chopped

2 tbsp mayonnaise

4 sesame buns, to serve

A handful of lettuce leaves, to serve

Sea salt and freshly ground pepper

Preheat your oven to 190°C/Gas 5. Halve the garlic bulb horizontally and roast for 25 mins on a baking tray till it's soft.

Whizz the bread in a food processor or coarsely grate to make breadcrumbs.

Scatter the breadcrumbs on a plate. Sprinkle the flour on a separate plate. Season. Whisk the egg in a shallow bowl.

Slice the hake fillets in half. Dip them in the flour, then egg and then breadcrumbs.

Remove the garlic from the oven and lay the breaded hake on the baking tray. Bake for 20 mins till golden.

Squeeze the garlic out of its skin and mash. Stir the garlic and parsley into the mayo.

Split the buns in half. Flash under the grill for a few mins to lightly toast them. Spread the bases with a little mayo. Top with a few lettuce leaves and the fish burgers. Top with the rest of the mayo.

THE Sauce

The simplest, most delicious fresh tomato sauce ever! Use for pizza, pasta, or as a base for Moroccan, Indian or other sauces, poach fish or meat in it – the kitchen's your oyster. Remember, the best-quality tomatoes will make the best sauce.

V · 5 MINS · 15-20 MINS · ROUGHLY 1KG OF SAUCE · 1 FOR 150G OF SAUCE

2kg tomatoes (any kind)

2 garlic cloves (more or less, to taste)

A handful of fresh basil, rosemary or any other herb you fancy, leaves only

1 tbsp olive oil

100ml red wine

2 tbsp balsamic vinegar

Sea salt and freshly ground pepper

Just toss everything into a food processor or blender. Blitz till smooth. It'll be quite pink at first.

Pour into a saucepan and gently boil till it's reduced to a lusciously thick, red sauce, about 15-20 mins. Add more seasoning, herbs, wine or balsamic if you think it needs it.

Amour Tatin Tomate

Did you know the French used to call tomatoes pommes d'amour, aka 'the love apple'? This inspired our Sorrel to make a savoury version of the French apple tart. Tomatoes are tumbled with thyme on a buttery pastry crust, with a cheesy twist.

(V) 🔪 20 MINS, PLUS 10 MINS' CHILLING/RESTING 🍳 45 MINS, PLUS 5 MINS' COOLING 🍴4 ❤1

2 tbsp olive oil

1 onion, thinly sliced

A handful of thyme, leaves only (see tip)

1 tbsp Demerara sugar

50g butter, cold

150g plain flour

100g Cheddar, grated

1 egg

2 tbsp ice-cold water

2 garlic cloves, thinly sliced

250g cherry tomatoes, halved

Sea salt and freshly ground pepper

Preheat your oven to 180°C/Gas 4. Heat 1 tbsp of the olive oil in a frying pan and add the onion. Season. Cook, stirring occasionally, on a very low heat for 15 mins till meltingly soft.

Add one-third of the thyme leaves to the onion and ½ tbsp of the sugar. Cook for 5 mins. Remove from the heat.

Grate the butter into a bowl. Add the flour, reserving 1 tbsp for later. Using your fingertips, rub the butter into the flour till it resembles breadcrumbs. Stir the Cheddar into the buttery flour and add half of the remaining thyme leaves. Season.

Separate the egg. Set the white aside. Add the yolk to the pastry, mix with the ice-cold water and bring together to form a dough. Add more water, 1 tsp at a time, if necessary but take care not to make it too wet.

Once you have a dough, roll into a ball and pop into the fridge for 10 mins to rest. Once it has rested, dust your work surface with the 1 tbsp of flour you saved earlier. Roll the dough into a circle slightly bigger than your small, round ovenproof pan or dish. It should be the thickness of a £1 coin.

Place your ovenproof pan on the hob. Add 1 tbsp of the olive oil and warm on a medium heat. Add the garlic slices and remaining thyme leaves and cook for 1 min till they sizzle. Add the remaining sugar and stir. Remove from the heat.

Arrange the tomatoes in the pan, cut-side down. If you have any extra, halve them again and place on top of the halves lining the pan. Spoon over the caramelised onions and spread evenly.

Place the pastry on top. Tuck the edges down into the sides. Brush with the egg white. Cook in the oven for 25 mins. Leave to cool for 5 mins. Flip out onto a plate. Serve with salad.

Thyme-saving Tip

To remove the thyme leaves quickly, poke the stems into the holes in a sieve and just pull them through the other side. The thyme leaves will be caught in the sieve.

Ginger & Tomato Baked Cod with Lime Courgetti

Spinning courgettes into noodles will never go out of fashion here, especially when paired with this smashing ginger-spiced sauce. Vegetarian and vegan friends: swap the cod for chickpeas or simply pair the veg noodles and sauce.

 15 MINS   15-20 MINS   4   2

3 courgettes

1 lime, zest and juice

3cm ginger, grated

3 garlic cloves, grated

1 chilli, deseeded and finely chopped

8 tomatoes, finely chopped

4 cod fillets

1 tbsp olive oil

4 shallots, thinly sliced

A handful of coriander, leaves only

Sea salt and freshly ground pepper

Preheat your oven to 180°C/Gas 4.

Make noodles or ribbons of courgette using a spiraliser, a julienne peeler or veg peeler. Stop when you get to the seeded middle. Finely chop the seeded middle and set aside. Put the noodles in a bowl.

Add the lime zest and juice to the courgette noodles, with a pinch of salt. Set aside to soak up the lime juice.

Mix the ginger, garlic and chilli with the tomatoes and the finely chopped courgette middles. Season.

Place the cod in a small baking dish. Pour the ginger tomatoes over the top. Slide into the oven and roast for 15-20 mins. When pierced with a sharp knife, the cod should be cooked through and flaky.

Meanwhile, heat a frying pan. When hot, add in the oil. Throw in the shallots and fry for 5 mins till golden and crispy.

Arrange a nest of courgette noodles on each plate. Top with the roasted cod. Spoon the sauce over the top. Scatter with the crispy shallots and coriander leaves.

Cooked Courgetti

We're serving our courgette noodles raw. If you fancy a softer bite, tip the noodles and lime juice into a wok or pan. Cook, stirring, for 2 mins and serve with the gingered cod.

Summer Bangers with Gremolata

Gremolata's just a fancy word for chopped parsley and garlic dazzled with lemon. This simple, healthy little supper can be balanced out with a crisp glass of white. Yin & yang, wine & bulgur wheat... Life is all about balance. Always use organic sausages to avoid an additive hangover.

 10 MINS 25 MINS 4 1

8 pork or veggie sausages

A couple of glosses of olive oil

A large handful of flat leaf parsley

2 garlic cloves

1 lemon, zest

4 large handfuls of cherry tomatoes, halved (or 6 big tomatoes cut into cherry tomato-sized chunks)

Sea salt and freshly ground pepper

Preheat your oven to 200°C/Gas 6. Pop a roasting or casserole dish in the oven to heat up. (Alternatively, fire up your barbecue.)

Tumble your sausages into the warmed oven dish with a gloss of oil. Or barbecue. Roast for 25 mins, or barbecue till blistered all over and cooked through, about 15-20 mins.

While the bangers bang, finely chop your parsley and garlic together. Grate in the lemon zest. Mix through, with a pinch of salt and pepper.

Halve your tomatoes. Season.

Once the bangers are cooked, mix them up with the halved tomatoes and a heap of gremolata. Taste. Add more gremolata if you like and a final gloss of oil.

Courgette & Mint Polpette

Polpette usually means meatballs, so of course, we've got an alternative take on the (green) matter. These vegan treats are great on their own, or go wild and have them with spaghetti, or even courgetti, tossed in olive oil, garlic and diced summer tomatoes.

 25 MINS 20 MINS 4 2

2 courgettes

400g tinned green lentils or chickpeas

2 garlic cloves, grated

A large handful of mint leaves, shredded

1 chilli, deseeded and finely chopped

1 tbsp tahini

1 lemon, zest

50g breadcrumbs

1 tbsp olive oil

Sea salt and freshly ground pepper

Preheat your oven to 200°C/Gas 6.

Coarsely grate the courgettes. Put in a sieve with a pinch of salt. Squeeze the courgettes a few times to get rid of some water, then leave in the sieve to drain while you prepare the rest of the polpette ingredients.

Drain and rinse the lentils or chickpeas. Shake dry. Tip into a large bowl and mash with a fork or masher. Add the garlic and mint leaves. Add half the chilli. Add the tahini and lemon zest.

Squeeze the courgettes again to get out any last liquid. Add to the bowl along with the breadcrumbs and some salt and pepper. Mix together to make a stiff mixture. Shape into 12 ping-pong sized balls.

Line a baking tray with baking paper. Spread the polpette out on the tray. Drizzle with the olive oil. Bake on the top shelf of the oven for 10 mins, then turn them over and bake for another 10 mins.

Sunny Spiced Courgette & Coconut Soup

Fresh turmeric is mind bogglingly good for you. (And really hard to find, unless you're an Abel & Cole-er.) This summer soup is so full of greatness you'll probably go out and save the world after just one bowl.

 10 MINS   15 MINS   4   1

1 chilli

2 tbsp cumin seeds

A couple of glosses of olive oil

3 garlic cloves, finely chopped

3cm turmeric, grated

3cm ginger, grated

400ml coconut milk

4 courgettes

A large handful of mint leaves

Up to 400ml water or veg stock

Crème fraîche or coconut milk, to garnish

Cut two or three thin slices from your chilli, more or less, to taste.

Heat a large dry frying pan over a low heat. Add your cumin seeds and toast for 1 min dry. Then add enough oil to just gloss your pan. Tumble the garlic, turmeric, ginger and chilli in with the cumin seeds. Cook for a few mins, till just softened. Add your coconut milk. Simmer for a few mins.

Wash your courgettes. Halve. Use a teaspoon to scoop out the soft, middle seeds (as you would with a cucumber – toss these bits into a salad or nibble them raw). Finely chop or grate the rest of the courgette. Add it to the pan. Cook for 1 min, just to soften.

Add the mint leaves. Blend till smooth, adding a little of the water or stock, if needed, to thin. Taste. Season as needed. Add more mint or ginger, as needed.

If you like heat, you can cut a few more slices from your chilli for a garnish. Fry in a little hot oil for a moment, just till they're turning crisp. Use to garnish the soup, along with a swirl of crème fraîche or coconut milk and a twist of black pepper.

Griddled Courgettes with Turmeric & Pickled Chilli

I bet you never thought you'd wake up craving courgettes. Well, give this gourd-geous recipe a bash and you'll be craving them day and night. It's ace with roast lamb, fried hake or daal and rice.

 10 MINS 20 MINS 4 1

3 large courgettes

A gloss or two of olive oil

75ml cider vinegar

2 tsp honey or agave syrup

1 red chilli, thinly sliced

2 tsp ground turmeric

Natural or coconut yogurt (optional)

Sea salt and freshly ground pepper

Trim off the woody top end of your courgettes. Using a large knife, slice the courgettes lengthwise into 0.5cm-thick panels (or, if you prefer, just slice into rounds).

Dust a little salt and pepper over the sliced courgettes. Gloss with a little bit of oil, but don't saturate them.

Warm the vinegar and honey in a little pan, just till the honey's dissolved. Swirl in your chilli slices. Take off the heat. Let them steep while you cook your courgettes.

Get a large frying or griddle pan smoking hot. Carefully arrange your courgette slices in a single layer. Cook till nicely charred on each side. You'll probably have to cook them in batches.

Once cooked, set on a cutting board and dust each layer with the ground turmeric. Repeat till all of your courgettes are used up.

Artfully arrange your turmeric-dusted courgettes on a platter or individual plates. Sprinkle with a little sea salt and pepper. Add a little gloss of oil, if needed and some drizzles of natural yogurt, too, if you fancy.

Dot the pickled chillies over the top. Save the pickling vinegar to make a salad dressing for big leafy green salad to serve alongside – simply shake the vinegar in a jam jar with an equal amount of olive oil and a pinch of salt.

Barbecued Watermelon, Feta & Walnut Salad

If you've never tried grilling a watermelon before, you'd better hop to it. It will blow your mind. Or, at least, your taste buds. So, light up the barbecue – or, if it's a typical British summer, a smoking hot frying pan will do.

 15 MINS 10 MINS 4 1

80g honey

2 limes, juice

A large pinch of dried chilli flakes

50g walnut halves

1 mini watermelon or ¼ of a larger one

Oil, for greasing

½ cucumber, finely diced

4 spring onions, thinly sliced

200g feta, crumbled

A handful of mint, leaves only, thinly sliced

Sea salt and freshly ground pepper

Light your barbecue. No BBQ? Just use a griddle pan or your oven grill set to high.

Whisk together the honey, lime juice and chilli flakes (use as much or as little as you like) with a pinch of salt and pepper, to make a smooth dressing. Set aside.

Toss the walnuts in a dry frying pan, toasting on a low heat till they smell nutty and are a little browned. Roughly chop. Set aside.

Halve the watermelon and chop it into 2cm-thick slices, then cut them into quarters.

Brush your griddle, grill pan or BBQ with a little neutral-tasting oil, like sunflower or vegetable oil. Thickly brush one side of the watermelon slices with half the honey dressing. Place them, sauce-side down, on the barbecue or grill pan. Cook for 3–5 mins till charred. While the watermelon cooks, brush the top side with more of the dressing. Flip the slices over and cook for another 3–5 mins.

Stack the watermelon slices on a serving plate. Scatter over the walnuts, cucumber, spring onions, feta and mint. Drizzle with any remaining honey dressing. Serve straight away.

Nectarine Ice

We're romancing the stone fruit with less work and less sugar in a thirst-quenching granite-sorbet hybrid.

Ⓥ 🔧 10 MINS, PLUS FREEZING 🍲 0 🍴 2-4 ♥ 1-2

4 nectarines (or peaches), stoned and cubed

Seeds from ½ vanilla pod

2-4 tbsp icing sugar

Spoons at the Ready

This is a make-and-eat-now dish. It isn't as nice when refrozen.

Halve the nectarines. Pop out the stones. Chop the nectarines and mix with the vanilla seeds. Freeze until solid, overnight or 2-3 hours if you arrange the vanilla-speckled fruit in a single layer on a baking tray or in a metal dish – it'll get cold faster.

Pop some serving glasses in the freezer 15 mins before serving.

Once the fruit is frozen, break up the pieces. Put them in a food processor with 2 tbsp of icing sugar. Whizz until it all starts coming together. It'll look icy and a bit like a granita but will start coming together like a sorbet when you scoop it out. Taste. Whizz in a bit more sugar, if needed.

Spoon the ice into chilled glasses. This will keep it icy for longer. It'll melt quickly so eat straight away.

Feisty Nectarine Relish

Spice up your life and a steak or roast aubergine while you're at it. Sweet and punchy, this relish transforms whatever it touches into something extra special.

 20 MINS 0 4 1

1 garlic clove, grated

25g ginger, grated

1 chilli, deseeded and chopped (or more, if you're a hothead/fire fan!)

1 lime, zest and juice

10g coriander, leaves only, finely chopped

3 ripe nectarines

1 tbsp caster sugar

Sea salt

Mix the garlic, ginger, chilli, lime zest and juice, and the chopped coriander together in a bowl.

Halve the nectarines. Pop out the stones. Chop the nectarines and stir into the relish with the sugar. Taste. Season with a little salt if you think it needs it. You can serve this relish straight away or keep it in the fridge for a few hours.

Hot Dogs with Beer & Mustard Onions

Helen Browning from the Soil Association is a pig farmer and makes ground-breaking, award-winning, organic hot dogs. Normal hot dogs are often full of rubbish, hers are full of nature, wisdom and flavour (and organic pork, obviously). If you can't get them, use organic bangers in this recipe instead.

 10 MINS   35 MINS   6   ½

3 red onions, sliced

25g butter

1 tsp olive oil

1 tsp yellow mustard seeds

1 tsp Demerara sugar

A handful of thyme, leaves only

100ml pale ale

3 demi baguettes or 1 large baguette

6 hot dogs or veggie sausages

Sea salt and freshly ground pepper

Preheat your oven to 200°C/Gas 6.

Put the onions in a pan with the butter and oil, and season. Cook and stir over a low heat for 10 mins.

Stir in the mustard seeds and Demerara sugar. Add the thyme leaves. Pour in the ale. Cover and simmer for 20 mins till the onions are soft.

While the onions cook, sprinkle the baguettes with a little water and bake till warmed through. Slice into six.

Heat your grill to high. Grill the hot dogs for 4–5 mins. Split the baguettes in half and pop in a hot dog. Top with mustardy onions.

Cherry & Amaretto Ripple Ice Cream

In the heat of the summer who has time to faff around churning ice cream? Not us. We've got weather to enjoy! This no-churn ice cream is remarkably easy and ridiculously delicious. Any cherries you don't immediately devour will soak up amaretto for a dish of a dessert.

(V) (prep) 30 MINS, PLUS AT LEAST 4 HRS' FREEZING (cook) 10-15 MINS (serves) 6 (heart) ½

For the cherry ripple:
250g cherries

2 tbsp amaretto

1 tbsp honey

2 tbsp water

For the ice cream:
1 vanilla pod

450ml double cream

100ml amaretto

1 tbsp honey

To serve:
250g cherries

A handful of mint leaves, finely shredded

Remove the stones from the cherries – just squeeze the cherries to pop out the stones, or halve and scoop them out with your fingers or a teaspoon. Place in a saucepan with the rest of the ripple ingredients.

Simmer on a gentle heat for 10-15 mins till the cherries have collapsed and the liquid is syrupy. Leave to chill. Blitz in a food processor or blender till smooth.

Halve the vanilla pod. Scrape out the seeds (keep the pod to add to a jar of sugar – this will infuse the flavour into the sugar).

Whip the double cream till it just forms soft peaks. Fold the amaretto, honey and vanilla seeds through the cream to incorporate them fully.

Pour the mix into a large, freezer-proof container. Spoon in the cherry puree. Gently ripple it through. Pop on a lid and place in the freezer for at least 4 hours.

Remove from the freezer 10-15 mins before serving. Scoop into bowls and serve with fresh cherries and finely shredded mint.

Naked Berries

It's a tough world out there for a little strawberry (and other delicate summer fruits), but organic farmers are clever and use companion planting, and naturally derived pest-deterrents like citronella and clove oil to shoo the pests away.

Non-organic farming employs a rather large army of chemical-based pesticides to keep their fruits safe. Alas, these can end up polluting water and the wider environment; they end up in food too, despite washing and cooking.

We like our berries naked. Or perhaps with a dollop of organic cream on the side.

Fantastic Frozen Strawberries with Warm White Choc & Cardamom Sauce

The first of the summer puddings. Seasonal frosty strawberries with warm cardamom white chocolate sauce is a simple stunner of a pud.

 V · 10 MINS, PLUS AT LEAST 1 HR FREEZING (UP TO OVERNIGHT) · 3-4 MINS · 4 · 1

500g strawberries (or a mix of strawberries, raspberries and blueberries)

100g white chocolate

Ground seeds from 3 cardamom pods

250ml double cream

Hull the strawberries. Spread out in a shallow roasting tin or baking tray with a lip (to stop the berries rolling everywhere). Freeze for at least 1 hour, up to overnight.

Chop the chocolate into small chunks. Tip into a small pan and pour in the double cream. Gently heat, stirring, till the chocolate has melted and formed a smooth sauce.

Divide the berries between four glasses or small bowls. Pour over the warm chocolate sauce to serve.

Choc-swap

Swap the white chocolate for dark chocolate and the cream for almond or coconut milk.

Strawberry & Prosecco Jam

Preserve the taste of summer berries with this wham-bam-thank-you strawberry jam. It's easy to make and even has a touch of Italian charm, thanks to a dash of Prosecco.

(V) 🔪 20 MINS 🍲 20-40 MINS 🍴 APPROX. 5 X 340G JARS

1kg strawberries

850g golden caster sugar

2 lemons, juice

250ml Prosecco

Put a saucer into the freezer to chill. Sterilise your jars by washing them in hot, soapy water and then drying them off in an oven set to 110°C/Gas ¼ or washing them in a dishwasher.

Hull the strawberries and set aside a handful of the smallest ones. Put the rest of them in a wide, heavy-based pan (a cast-iron casserole dish or preserving pan is a good option). Use a masher or fork to mash the strawberries together.

Add the sugar, lemon juice and Prosecco to the pan. Add the whole strawberries.

Gently heat the pan to melt the sugar. Turn the heat up and bring it to the boil. Boil for 20-40 mins till the jam is set. Check after 20 mins by taking the saucer out of the freezer and putting 1 tsp of jam on it. Leave it to cool for 1 min, then push it with your finger. If it wrinkles a little, the jam is ready (strawberry jam will set quite softly, so it won't be very thick or solid). Keep boiling the jam and testing every few mins till you get the little wrinkle.

Take the jam off the heat. Let it cool for 5-10 mins. Skim off any pink scum.

Ladle the jam into the sterilised jars. Seal. The jam will keep well in the jars for up to a year. Once opened, store in the fridge and eat within 1 month.

Strawberry Cheesecake Yogurt

You'll have this pud ready faster than you can say 'cheesecake yogurt'. That is if you say it for 15 mins straight or thereabouts. Seriously though, this one is easy as pie.

 V 🥄 15 MINS, PLUS 15 MINS' MARINATING 🍲 0 🍴 6 ❤ 1

500g strawberries, hulled

2 tbsp caster sugar

300g vanilla yogurt

300g cream cheese

10 digestive biscuits, crumbled

Pop the strawberries in a lidded container. Sprinkle with the sugar. Mix. Leave to marinate for 15 mins. The sugar draws out the strawberry juices, which makes a gorgeous syrup.

Fold the yogurt and cream cheese together.

Roughly chop the strawberries. Layer them in a serving bowl with the yogurt and cream cheese mix and the digestives. Drizzle with a bit of the strawberry juices. Let it sit for a few mins so the biscuits go a little bit soft.

To make them pretty and easy to tote to a picnic, layer the crushed biscuits, cheesecake yogurt and berries in individual jam jars.

Dancing on the Job

We've been working with organic vintners (the fancy term for wine makers) for well over a decade and every weekend gives us an opportunity to test a hypothesis: organic wine doesn't give you a hangover.

A few people reckon there's something to this hangover theory. Non-organic grapes are in fact, one of the most heavily sprayed crops.

That aside, we believe drinking organic wine is more interesting because you can taste the place, or 'terroir'. Try an organic sancerre, for instance, and you can taste if it comes from chalky or clay soil. Amazing, huh?

Many organic vines are still harvested by hand too, which means more jobs for the local community. We'll drink to that.

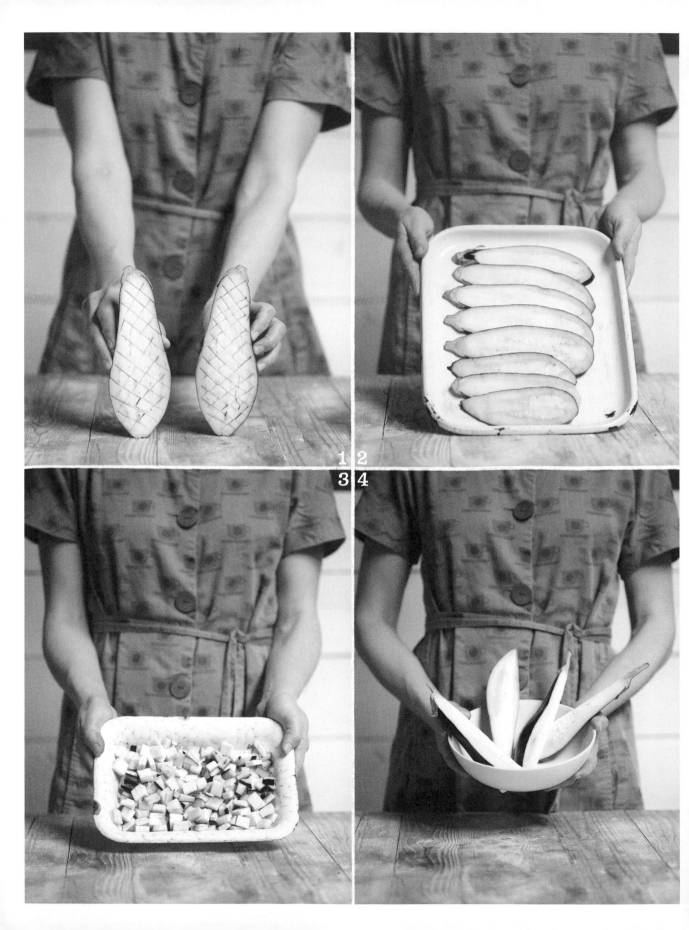

1 2
3 4

Mediterranean Aubergine & Herb Salad

Finely diced aubergine and red pepper, roasted until golden, tossed with heaps of fragrant herbs and crowned with the most delicious garlic and herb ewes' cheese... This salad is as much fun as the Nice Carnival.

 **V** OR **Vg** 🥄 20 MINUTES 🍳 25 MINUTES 🍴4 ♡2

3 aubergines, cut into 1cm dice

2 red peppers, deseeded and cut into 1cm dice

A few drizzles of olive oil

2 garlic cloves, finely chopped

3 tbsp balsamic vinegar

A handful of basil leaves, finely chopped

A handful of flat leaf parsley leaves, finely chopped

A handful of chives, finely chopped

200g soft, crumbly goats' or ewes' cheese*

Sea salt and freshly ground pepper

Preheat your oven to 220°C/Gas 7. Set a large roasting tray on the top shelf to heat up.

Tumble the diced aubergine and pepper onto the warmed roasting tray. Add a good drizzle of olive oil. Season well. Roast for 20-25 minutes or until golden around the edges, turning the veg halfway through.

Remove from the oven and stir the garlic through the roasted veg, along with the balsamic vinegar. Return to the oven for 5 minutes.

Add the finely chopped herbs to the veg and toss together. Pile onto plates. Crumble or thinly slice the cheese and dot it over the top.

Finish with a crack of pepper and a drizzle of olive oil.

Swap with toasted pine nuts for a vegan option.

1. Criss-cross

Halve your aubergine and make 1cm-deep slashes about 1cm apart in one direction. Repeat in the opposite direction. Rub with oil. Dust with spice. Roast in a 180°C/Gas 4 oven until golden and tender, about 30 mins.

2. Aubergine steaks

Cut into 1cm-thick panels (or you can do rounds). Set a large frying pan over high heat. Dust the aubergines with salt. Place in the pan, in a single layer, no oil needed. Cook till charred, about 3 mins, on each side.

3. Aubergine croutons

Slice into panels as in Step 2. Then finely dice. Toss with oil and spice (garam masala is nice). Fry or roast in a 180°C/Gas 4 oven till golden and a little crisp. Delicious with chickpeas, herbs and a dollop of yogurt.

4. Wedges

Cut the aubergines into 4 wedges. Rub with oil, salt and pepper. Cook in a smoking-hot pan on each side until lightly charred and tender, roast in a 180°C/Gas 4 oven or grill. Lovely with a tahini or feta dressing.

Smoky Aubergine & Tahini Chocolate Brownies

Aubergine? Brownies? Stick with us! This is genius, if a little bonkers. These rich, organic beauties have a dense, fudgy texture and sophisticated flavour. Gorge-pots warm or cold with vanilla ice cream.

 (V) 20 MINS, PLUS 15 MINS' COOLING   35 MINS   12   ¼

2 aubergines, weighing 500g

100g unsalted butter, softened, plus extra for greasing

200g dark chocolate

3 medium eggs

200g honey

60g cocoa powder

100g ground almonds

125g tahini

Sea salt

If you have a gas hob, turn on a medium-sized ring and set it to low. Place the aubergines directly on the flame. Char all over till blackened and tender. Alternatively, halve the aubergines and grill, skin-side up, for 10 mins or till blackened. Pop in a bowl. Leave to cool for 10–15 mins.

Preheat your oven to 190°C/Gas 5. Grease a brownie pan with a little butter.

Break the chocolate into small chunks. Tip into a heatproof bowl and set it over a pan of simmering water – make sure the water doesn't touch the bowl. Heat for 2–3 mins till the chocolate has melted. Or, if you have a microwave, you can melt it in there, checking every 15–20 secs to make sure it doesn't burn.

Peel the blackened skin off. Place the aubergine flesh and seeds in a clean bowl. Add the butter and beat together till combined. Crack in the eggs and beat them in, then add the honey. Beat till well mixed. Pour in the melted chocolate and beat again till everything is well combined.

Sift in the cocoa powder. Add the ground almonds with a pinch of salt. Stir together till mixed. Pour the batter into the tin, making sure to scrape everything in.

Spoon the tahini into the brownie mixture, dolloping it in across the tin, then use a skewer to swirl it around a little so you get a marbled effect. Bake for 25 mins till a crust has just formed and the middle still has a wobble in it. If you have a big roasting tin, add a few handfuls of ice to that and sit the hot brownie tin on the ice. Pour in cold water so it doesn't come above the tin – this ice bath will immediately stop the brownies cooking further, so you keep the soft, gooey middle. Leave them to cool.

You can serve the brownies warm, or let them cool completely, then freeze for 1 hr or overnight – this helps to make the texture really fudgy. Take them out of the freezer 1 hr before serving, then slice into 12 pieces, and serve by themselves or with a scoop of vanilla ice cream. They'll keep for 7 days in an airtight tin or you can freeze them for up to 3 months.

Ginger Melon Smoothie

It's smoothie sailing with this summer-fresh organic melon and zingy lime and ginger drink.

 10 MINS ▢ 0 🍴 2-4 ♡ 1

1 melon
3cm piece ginger
1 lime, zest and juice
A handful of mint leaves
A large glassful of ice

Peel and deseed the melon. Cut into chunks. Peel the ginger and cut into small pieces. Place all the ingredients in a high-speed blender. Blitz.

Apricot Bellinis

When apricot season starts, embrace it, it really is a treat. This is our stunning, honey-kissed twist on the classic peachy Italian fizz.

 10 MINS ▢ 0 🍴 4-6

4 ripe apricots
2 tbsp honey
1 bottle of chilled Prosecco

Halve and stone the apricots. Blend with the honey. Taste. Whip more honey into the mix, if needed. Pass through a sieve to give you a smooth puree.

Spoon 2 tbsp of the honeyed apricot puree into each champagne glass. Top up with chilled Prosecco. If you have leftover puree, it will keep in the fridge for 3–4 days or you can freeze it for up to 6 months.

Virgin Bellini

Top up with elderflower fizz or use more apricot puree and just top up with sparkling water.

Watermelon Mojito Lollies

A classic mojito shaken with fresh watermelon and frozen for a refreshing, boozy summer cooler. These are very grown-up lollies indeed.

 10 MINS   FREEZING TIME: 24 HOURS   8

100ml white rum

3 limes, zest and juice

2 tbsp agave syrup

4 mint sprigs and a handful of small mint leaves

600g watermelon

Pour the rum and lime juice into a small pan. Add the agave syrup and lime zest. Bring to a bubble, then immediately remove from the heat. Throw in the mint sprigs and leave to infuse and cool.

Cut the watermelon into segments and carve off the skin. Remove the seeds. Chuck into a food processor and whizz till smooth. Pass through a sieve into a jug. You should have about 500ml of watermelon juice.

When the rum and lime mix is cool, pluck out the mint sprigs and discard. Stir in the watermelon juice. Taste and add a little more agave syrup if you think it needs it. The lollies will taste less sweet once frozen.

Pour into lolly moulds and poke in a few small mint leaves. Insert sticks (depending on your lolly mould). Pop into the freezer for at least 24 hrs. Remove from the moulds and enjoy straight away.

Elderflower & Strawberry Power Pressé

Adventure time! We're off to forage as this summery elixir is pretty much free to make. Low in sugar, it is full of elderflower power as the flowers are infused in cold water, which captures the fresh scent of summer. Master this, then use the same steps with rose petals, honeysuckle or jasmine. Stick a feather in your cap and add 'Foraged Drink Supremo' to your CV.

 20 MINS, PLUS OVERNIGHT STEEPING 5 MINS 6-8

200g strawberries (or cherries, or gooseberries)

20-25 elderflower heads

1 lemon

1 ltr cold water

Caster sugar, to taste

Shake the flower heads to remove any bugs (the truly sustainable protein).

Pluck the flowers from the stalks and stems (do it by hand and you'll get a richer flavour and less stalk, though scissors do the job just fine).

Scoop the flowers into a sieve to help liberate any further insects. Tumble into a large bowl.

With a veg peeler or zester, peel your lemon to get strips and add to the bowl. Squeeze in all the juice. Pour in the cold water.

Place a little sheet of baking paper over the top to lock in all the flavour, to keep it from browning and to keep anything else from diving in! Steep for 8 hrs or overnight.

Trim the strawberries or gooseberries or, if using cherries, remove stems and stones. Add to the elderflower. Blend everything together.

Strain through a muslin cloth or tea towel-lined sieve into a large saucepan. Squeeze the flowers to ensure you get as much flavour out of them as possible.

Gently warm through. Add a few spoons or shakes of sugar to sweeten to your liking. Serve on ice straight away or bottle, cork/ seal and store in the fridge for up to a week. Freeze any excess for up to 6 months.

You're a Real Wild One

The rules of foraging: Leave enough for nature (the wildlife loves elderflower too), the plant itself and other foragers. Picking all the flowers means no berries in the autumn. The best time to pick is when it's sunny and warm. Check the forager's code before you go and abide by it whenever you embark on a foraging adventure.

Gooseberry Lemonade

Summer isn't summer without an ice-filled jug of lemonade. Learn this simple and delicious recipe and you'll be sipping our super lemonade all summer long.

 10 MINS 0 1 LITRE 1

2 lemons, plus extra slices to serve

150g gooseberries

1 ltr water

4 tbsp sugar, honey or agave syrup

½ vanilla pod (optional)

Halve your lemons. Grate the lemon zest into a blender. Add the lemon juice, straining out the pips. Trim the gooseberries. Add. Blend with the water. Strain into a bowl through a fine mesh sieve or muslin.

Stir in the sugar, honey or agave syrup. Add half a vanilla pod, if you like, for a hint of vanilla.

Pour the juice into a jug. Give it a good stir. Taste. Add more sugar, honey or agave syrup, if you like.

Chill with ice or in the fridge till ready to serve. Garnish with lemon slices. Freeze any leftovers as ice lollies.

Abel & 'Bena

During the Second World War kids were given blackcurrant cordial for free because it was 'full of Vit C'. This homemade version has all the goodness, without the sugar.

10 MINS 10 MINS 200ML ½

225g blackcurrants or blackberries

200ml water

4 tbsp honey or agave syrup

Pluck your blackcurrants from their stalks. Place in a saucepan.

Add the water. Set the pan over a medium heat. Bring the blackcurrants to the boil – you'll start to see the water bubble up. Lower the heat. Simmer for 10 mins.

Press the blackcurrant mixture through a sieve or through a damp, clean tea towel into a bowl. Squeeze as much juice out of the currants as possible. Compost the skins.

Stir the honey or agave syrup into the currant juice. Taste. Add more agave syrup, if needed, till it's as sweet as you like it.

Store in a jam jar in the fridge till ready to use. When ready to serve, pour into glasses or a jug and top up with water – as much or as little as you like. Just add a little, taste, and keep trickling the water in till it's just right.

RIDICULOUSLY QUICK RECIPES

Elderflower Soaked Berries

Toss hulled and quartered strawberries and/or whole raspberries with a drop of elderflower cordial for a wonderfully impressive (and incredibly quick) pudding or breakfast pancake topping.

Grilled Nectarines with Amaretto Mascarpone

Serve fresh or grilled nectarine halves with a tub of mascarpone whipped with 1–2 tbsp of amaretto and a drizzle of honey. To grill the nectarines, just arrange halved and stoned nectarines, cut-side up, on a grill pan with a sprinkle of sugar, if you like, and grill on the highest setting till tender and lightly charred.

Lettuce Dippers

The fastest and easiest – and extremely delicious – way to eat a lettuce is to treat it like a crudité. Simply quarter and dip – gorgeous with a simple houmous or our buttermilk dressing on page 155. Roll up larger, softer leaves before dipping (pop a carrot or cucumber stick in the middle for extra crunch).

Melon Salad Bowl

Halve your melon (any kind) and remove the seeds. Use a large spoon to scoop out all the melony flesh, reserving the shell. Chop the flesh into chunks. Toss with rocket or other salad leaves and herbs like mint. Dress with a little olive oil, lime zest and juice. Pile into your halved melon shells. Finish with a crumbling of feta and a sprinkling of chopped pistachios.

Tahini Aubergine Wedges

One of the fastest and easiest ways to prep an aubergine is to quarter it into wedges. Once you've got your wedges, set a large frying pan over a high heat. Cook the aubergine wedges on all sides till nicely charred. Season well. Spritz with lemon juice. Drizzle with tahini yogurt (made by mixing 1 tbsp tahini with 2 tbsp yogurt, 1 tsp lemon juice and 1 tsp honey or maple syrup). Finish with a pinch of chilli and fresh herbs.

Tomato Dip Dabs

Dust a plate with a sprinkling of ground cumin and a pinch of salt. Halve your tomatoes. Dab the cut side in the spice, and eat. Add some toasted sesame seeds to the mix, too, if you like.

AUTUMN

Welly boots, ruby roots and bonfire soot.
The UK is bursting at the seams with gorgeous fruit and veg.
Celebrate apples and savour sweetcorn.
Walk in the early morning mist, build a bonfire, bang
a conker and hug an organic pumpkin.

Seasonal Stars

Sweetcorn, squash, broccoli, cauliflowers,
apples, potatoes, swede, pears, plums

Butter-Roasted Sweetcorn

The corn is as high as an elephant's eye (approximately eight foot or so) so enjoy it at its seasonal best. This genius trick will give you cobs that are as golden and impressive-looking as a beautiful mornin'.

(V) 🔧 10 MINS 🍳 30 MINS 🍴 4 ❤️ 1

4 sweetcorn cobs

2-3 tbsp butter

Sea salt and freshly ground pepper

Preheat your oven to 220°C/Gas 7.

Strip the husks on your sweetcorn, but keep them attached to the base. Remove any damaged-looking husks but leave the rest intact. Yank out the silky threads, leaving you with smooth cobs.

Melt the butter in a saucepan. Brush or slather the melted butter all over the cobs. Season well. Wrap the cobs up in their husks. Twist the tops of the husks together to help secure – or tie up with one or two of the discarded husks or some butcher's string. Set in a roasting tin and roast for 30 mins or so till the cobs are fully tender.

Strip the husks back and start eating.

BUNDLES OF JOY

Fresh Corn Polenta with Peperonata

When that Indian summer has finally come to a close, soak up some Italian sunshine instead with this Peperonta – a sweet red Italian pepper stew. Even better, it's gorgeous with fresh organic sweetcorn polenta.

 **V** • 15 MINS • 30 MINS • 4 • 3

6 sweetcorn cobs

1 tbsp olive oil

1 onion, chopped

2 red peppers, deseeded and roughly chopped

1 garlic clove, crushed

500g cherry tomatoes, roughly chopped

80g black olives, pitted

A handful of thyme, leaves only

300ml boiling water

3 tbsp butter

Sea salt and freshly ground pepper

Pull the husks and silky threads off the sweetcorn cobs. Stand the cobs upright on a board. Run a knife down the sides to slice off the kernels. Chuck the kernels in a pan with a pinch of salt. Set aside.

Warm the olive oil in a deep frying pan or wok over a low heat. Add the onion. Season with salt and pepper. Fry for 5-8 mins till soft, stirring often.

Add the peppers to the frying pan. Fry for 3-4 mins till they start to soften. Add the garlic, tomatoes, olives and half the thyme leaves. Cook over a high heat for 5 mins, then turn the heat down and gently cook for 15 mins till thick. This is your peperonata.

Pour the boiling water over the sweetcorn kernels. Cover. Put on a high heat and bring to the boil. Turn the heat down and simmer for 5 mins. Drain the sweetcorn over a heatproof jug so you save the cooking water. Return the sweetcorn to the pan.

Add the butter to the pan and 50ml of the cooking water. Use a handheld blender to blitz the sweetcorn into a rough purée. No blender? Ladle the corn into a food processor with a little cooking water and pulse till you get the consistency you want. Or, mash the corn in a bowl with a masher – you won't need to add extra water. Taste and season. Gently reheat the polenta over a low heat till hot. Add a little more cooking water if it's too thick.

Spoon the sweetcorn polenta into two bowls. Top with the peperonata and the rest of the thyme leaves.

Pattipan Squash Stuffed with Sweetcorn & Feta

Celebrate the sunniest of autumn stars with this properly wowy veggie centrepiece. Pattipan squash look like little UFOs, which is fitting as this sweetcorn and squash recipe is out of this world.

 V 40 MINS 55 MINS 4 2

6-8 pattipan squash, weighing 300g each (see tip)

1 sweetcorn cob

A splash of olive oil

1 small onion, finely chopped

½ tsp mixed spice

½ tsp paprika

A pinch of chilli powder

100g feta cheese

1 egg yolk

100ml whole milk

A handful of sage leaves

A knob of butter

Sea salt and freshly ground pepper

Preheat your oven to 180°C/Gas 4. Slice the tops off the pattipans, about a quarter of the way down, to form lids. Scoop out and discard the seeds. Scoop out the flesh from the lids and bases, leaving a 0.5cm wall of squash behind.

Finely chop the pattipan flesh. Pull the husks and silky threads off the sweetcorn cob. Stand the cob upright on a board. Run a knife down the sides to slice off the kernels.

Warm a splash of olive oil in a large pan over a very low heat. Add the onion. Season. Cover and cook for 10 mins till soft but not coloured. Stir often.

Tip the chopped squash into the pan. Cover and cook for another 10 mins till the squash has started to soften. Chuck in the sweetcorn and cook for another 5 mins till everything is tender.

Stir the mixed spice and paprika into the veg with a pinch of chilli powder. Crumble in most of the feta and stir well. Taste and add more salt, pepper or spices if you think it needs it.

Beat the egg and milk in a bowl, then season.

Place the hollowed-out pattipans in a roasting tin. Spoon in the veg mix, dividing it equally between the squash. Spoon over the milk and egg mix. Cover the pattipans with their lids. Bake in the oven for 30 mins till they're tender all the way through.

Fry the sage leaves in a little butter till crisp. Serve scattered over the cooked squashes.

For Larger Flying Saucers

You can use bigger pattipan squash but they will need longer to cook. Roughly increase the cooking time by weight, so if a 300g squash needs 30 mins to cook through once stuffed, aim for 1 hr for a 600g squash or 45 mins for a 450g squash.

Broccoli Slaw with Red Thai Yogurt & Toasted Cashews

Did you know you can eat broccoli raw? What a talented tree lookalike! This coleslaw is next-level healthy, with some pretty special guest stars like kefir, if you can find it, which is full of good-for-your-gut bacteria.

 15 MINS 5 MINS 4 1

1 broccoli head

1 lime, zest and juice

1 tbsp olive or coconut oil

2 garlic cloves, thinly sliced

A large handful of cashews

2 tsp red Thai curry paste (or more or less, to taste)

250g natural or coconut yogurt, or kefir

A handful of fresh mint, parsley and/or coriander leaves, chopped

Sea salt

Trim the woody end from the broccoli stem. Quarter the broccoli, then thinly slice. Bring a pot of salted water to the boil. Add the broccoli and cook for 1 min. Drain and rinse under cold water to stop it cooking further. Toss in a bowl with a pinch of salt and the zest and juice from your lime.

Heat a small frying pan and add the olive or coconut oil. Toast the garlic and cashews over a medium heat, constantly turning, till golden. Remove from the pan. Save the oil for your dressing.

Ripple the curry paste through the yogurt. If serving on a platter, you can create a bed of red-Thai-rippled yogurt for the broccoli to sit on, or simply mix the yogurt with the broccoli or dollop it on top. Whichever way you choose, finish with the cashews, crispy garlic and a sprinkling of the herbs.

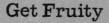

Get Fruity

Give this slaw even more flare by adding little nuggets of fresh pineapple to the mix.

Broccoli Walnut Rarebit

Well, this is a rare treat. Ditch the toast and bring on the veg! This is easy to make and insanely delicious. The cidery cheese sauce complements the earthy walnuts, which both go beautifully with the texture and flavour of the broccoli.

(V) 🥄 10 MINS 🍲 15 MINS 🍴 2 AS A VEGGIE MAIN (A COSY DISH FOR SHARING) ❤ 1

1 broccoli head

1 tbsp butter

1 tbsp plain white flour

150ml cider

150g Cheddar, grated

2 tsp Dijon mustard

A pinch of chilli powder

A handful of chopped walnuts

Sea salt and freshly ground pepper

Preheat the grill to high. No grill? Preheat your oven to 220°C/Gas 7.

Get a pot of salted water on to boil. Trim a good bit off the stem of your broccoli. Compost the stalk. Plunge your broccoli into the boiling water. Cook for 3–5 mins, or till just tender but still bright green. Drain and tip into a bowl of ice-cold water.

Put your now-empty pan back on the heat. Add the butter. As soon as it's melted, swirl in the flour. Whisk to a smooth paste.

Whisk in the cider, little by little, until you have a sauce consistency. Heap in the cheese. Stir till melted. Fold in the mustard, the chilli powder and some black pepper. Taste. Tweak seasoning as needed.

Put your broccoli head in a baking dish. Spoon the cidery cheese sauce over your broccoli. Scatter with the walnuts. Cook on a high shelf in the oven till the cheese is golden and bubbly, 10–15 mins.

Hands Up Who Loves Bacon?

For a long time, all bacon was dry cured. This traditional process takes time. Each cut of pork is rubbed with a salt mix that draws the flavour out of the meat and preserves it. It's then cured for at least 5 days and is then dry-cured for up to 20 days before being ready.

Unfortunately, most mass produced bacon is wet-cured these days. This involves soaking or injecting the pork with a solution that quickly changes it into bacon.

Sounds like a shortcut? It is.

We believe in food made the right way, and when it comes to curing, time equals flavour. And we love flavour.

Bacon & Sage Frittata with Warm Cannellini Bean Salad

It's bacon, eggs and beans, but not as you know them. An Italian-inspired dish complete with crispy, fried lardons, golden-yolked organic eggs and creamy cannellini beans. It'll be enough to have you planning your own Tuscan getaway.

15 MINS　20 MINS　4　3

1 red onion, thinly sliced

2 tbsp red wine vinegar

400g chestnut mushrooms

400g cherry tomatoes

A handful of sage leaves

½ tbsp olive oil

250g lardons

8 eggs

400g tin of cannellini beans

2 large handfuls of baby leaf spinach

Sea salt and freshly ground pepper

Pop the onion into a bowl and pour over the red wine vinegar. Add a pinch of salt and mix. Leave to marinate while you prepare the vegetables.

Thickly slice the mushrooms. Chop the tomatoes into quarters. Thinly slice the sage leaves.

Warm a large ovenproof frying pan over a medium heat for 1 min. Add the oil. Tip in the lardons. Cook, stirring, for 4-5 mins till they start to crisp up and turn golden.

Add half the marinated onions to the pan, along with all of the mushrooms and half of the tomatoes. Cook for 4-5 mins, stirring occasionally, till the veg are soft.

Crack the eggs into a bowl. Beat together with a good crack of black pepper and most of the sage. Pour the egg mixture into the pan and cook. Turn your grill on and set it to medium-high.

Cook the frittata on the hob for 3 mins till the base has set. Then slide it under the grill and cook for 5 mins till bubbling and firm. Remove and leave to cool slightly.

Drain and rinse the beans. Tip them into a pan with the remaining marinated onions and tomatoes. Cook on a medium heat for 3-4 mins till warmed through. Tip in the spinach and stir together until just wilted. Taste and add salt and pepper if you think it needs it. Serve the frittata in slices alongside the warm bean salad.

You Say Frittata...

We say fried – that's what frittata means in Italian. It's a chunky, open-faced omelette that can include all sorts of ingredients. If you have any of your frittata left over, it will keep for 3 days in the fridge. Lovely cold or sandwiched between two pieces of hot, buttered sourdough toast.

Pulled Pumpkin

Grab your coat, you've pulled... pumpkin. You'll be pulling like a pro before the end of this one and what makes it a dream is the fact that it's easy as pie.

 10 MINS · 30 MINS · 4 · 1

1 pumpkin

A drizzle of olive oil

A handful of fresh thyme, leaves only

1 chilli, finely chopped

Barbecue sauce

Sea salt and freshly ground pepper

4-6 burger buns or rolls, to serve

Coleslaw, to serve

Preheat your oven to 200°C/Gas 6.

Halve your pumpkin horizontally and scoop out the seeds. Rub the inside all over with oil, then season with salt and pepper. Place your seasoned pumpkin, cut side up, on a baking tray on the top shelf of your oven and roast for 30 mins.

After 30 mins (or when all the moisture has been cooked off), the flesh should be rich and dense.

Pull the flesh and toss in a bowl with thyme, chilli and barbecue sauce. Serve in a bun with crunchy slaw.

Squash & Tahini Soup with Pomegranate

A tickle of cumin, the smooth velvetiness of a creamy onion squash and the nutty bite of tahini. It all makes for one fine bowl of edible central heating, especially when it's adorned with jewels... Ahem, pomegranate seeds!

 15 MINS 20 MINS 4 1½

1 onion squash

1 tbsp olive oil

1 onion, finely chopped

1 garlic clove, finely chopped

2 tsp ground cumin

2 tbsp tahini

1 veg stock cube or 750ml homemade veg stock

1 pomegranate

Sea salt and freshly ground pepper

Halve your squash. Scoop out the seeds. Chop the squash into small chunks, skin and all. Warm a large pan over a high heat for 1 min. Add the oil to the pan. Add the squash and onion. Season well.

Cook the veg over a medium–high heat for 15 mins till tender and a little caramelised at the edges. Add the garlic to the pan with the cumin and tahini. Sizzle for 1 min. Crumble in your stock cube and add 750ml of boiling water (or use homemade stock). Simmer for 5 mins or till the squash is mashably tender.

Blend till smooth. Simmer to thicken the soup a little further, if you wish. Season to taste, adding more cumin, if needed.

Halve your pomegranate. Hold it skin-side up in the palm of your hand over a bowl. Whack the back with a wooden spoon and the seeds should fall through your fingers. Sprinkle the seeds over your soup - be generous as they really add dazzle to the taste and texture to the soup.

Roast Cauli & Cashew Biryani

We love one-pot food because it means less washing up and more time for after-dinner parlour games. Or dancing. Or vegging out. This classic Indian dish is perfect with roast cauli and the rice soaks up all the lovely spices.

 20 MINS 45 MINS 4 2

300g white basmati rice

2 tbsp olive oil

1 cauliflower, broken into small florets

2 leeks, finely sliced

1 veg stock cube

5cm ginger, grated

1-2 chillies, finely chopped

1 bay leaf

1 cinnamon stick

6 cloves

2 tsp mild curry powder

650ml boiling water

100g spinach

A handful of cashews, to serve

Yogurt, to serve (optional)

Sea salt and freshly ground pepper

Preheat your oven to 220°C/Gas 7. Rinse the rice and set aside.

Pour the olive oil into a shallow ovenproof casserole dish or roasting tin. Slide it into the oven to heat for 2 mins. Add the cauliflower and leeks to the casserole dish. Toss to coat in the oil. Season. Roast for 20 mins.

Crumble the stock cube into a heatproof jug. Add the ginger and chilli, along with the bay leaf, cinnamon stick, cloves and spice mix. Add the boiling water to the jug and stir.

Turn the oven down to 180°C/Gas 4.

Stir the rice into the dish of veg. Pour in the spiced stock. Season. Cover. Bake for 25 mins till the stock is absorbed.

Roughly chop the cashews. Fish the bay leaf, cinnamon stick and cloves out of the rice. Taste and add more salt and pepper if you think it needs it. Fork in the spinach to just wilt it.

Serve topped with the chopped cashews and spoonfuls of yogurt, if you like.

Jolly Roast Cauli

Cauliflower is often an underrated veg. Delicious and filling, yet low in calories, it's veritably versatile. Sometimes we serve this Spanish-inspired cracker at Halloween and pretend it's zombie brains in 'blood' sauce.

 V 🥄 20 MINS 🍲 1 HR 🍴 4 ♡ 3

1 cauliflower, approximately 800g

650ml hot veg stock

75ml + 1 tbsp olive oil

1 lemon, juice

1 tsp black peppercorns

1 bay leaf

A few thyme sprigs

1 tsp dried chilli flakes

2 red peppers

1 small onion, finely chopped

2 garlic cloves, crushed

1 tsp smoked paprika

300ml passata

Sea salt and freshly ground pepper

Preheat your oven to 200°C/Gas 6. Put a heatproof dish or bowl full of water in the bottom of the oven (this will turn to steam and help keep your 'brains'/cauliflower moist).

Slice the leaves off the cauliflower and slice the base so it sits flat. Pour the vegetable stock, 75ml of oil and lemon juice into a pan large enough to fit the whole cauliflower. Add a pinch of sea salt, the peppercorns, bay leaf, thyme sprigs and chilli flakes. Lower in the cauliflower, cut-side up. Cover, bring to the boil and then simmer for 15 mins till the cauliflower is tender when you push in a skewer.

While the cauliflower simmers, start making the 'blood' sauce. If you have a gas hob, lay the peppers directly on the hob, set to a medium flame. Char for 15–20 mins, using tongs to turn them so they are blackened all over. Set aside and let them cool for 15 mins. No gas hob? Char the peppers under the grill.

Drain the cauliflower. Discard the herbs and spices. Place the cauliflower, cut-side down, in a baking tray. Slide into the oven and roast for 25–30 mins till the cauliflower is a little browned all over.

While the peppers cool and the cauli roasts, warm a pan on a medium heat, then add the onion and 1 tbsp of oil. Season and fry for 5 mins, stirring, till the onion has softened. Stir the garlic into the onion with the smoked paprika and passata. Cover and simmer for 8–10 mins to mingle the flavours.

Peel the black skin off the peppers. Halve them, scoop out the seeds and white bits. Roughly chop them and add to the pan. Use a handheld blender to blitz the sauce till smooth, or blitz it in a blender or food processor. Taste and adjust the seasoning.

Spoon the red pepper sauce ('blood') onto a serving plate with a lip. Carefully place the roast cauliflower ('brains') in the middle of the plate. Serve straight away, carving everyone slices.

Head-to-Stalk Eating

Don't throw your cauliflower leaves away. Think of them as a free cabbage and cook them much the same. Super stir-fried, but even better roasted with sea salt and a gloss of oil or a slick of butter.

A Game of Tagine

This wonderful recipe uses our fantastic game pie mix. Seasonal wild game is ethical and tastes sensational. We've given two different serving suggestions below, so you've got three recipes in one!

 15 MINS 45 MINS 4 1, 2 IF SERVED IN A SQUASH

A little oil or butter

500g game pie mix, available seasonally from Abel & Cole, or mix your own

1 onion, thinly sliced

1 tbsp freshly grated ginger

2 tsp ground cinnamon

2 tsp ground cumin

2 tsp ground coriander

A pinch of chilli powder

1 orange, zest and juice

2 garlic cloves, finely chopped

6 dates, halved and pitted

400g tin of chopped tomatoes

500ml water

1 sweet potato

A handful of mint or parsley leaves, chopped, to serve

Sea salt and freshly ground pepper

Heat a little oil or butter in a large pan. Add the game pie mix and fry for 5-10 mins till golden all over. Season well. Add the onion to the pan and fry with the game for about 5 mins till tender.

Swirl in the ginger, spices, orange zest and juice. Add the garlic, dates, tomatoes and water to the pan. Simmer for 30 mins or till the meat is really tender and the sauce thickens.

Meanwhile, peel and grate in your sweet potato. Bring to the boil. Cook for 5-10 mins till everything is thick and rich. Taste and tweak the spices and seasoning. Finish by scattering over a handful of chopped mint or parsley.

Squash Cauldron

To serve the tagine, try popping it inside two roasted onion squashes. Just cut the top off each squash and scoop out the seeds. Rub the inside with a little oil, salt and pepper. Roast on a baking tray on the top shelf of a preheated oven, at 220°C/Gas 7, for about 40 mins till tender. Fill with the tagine and serve.

Yogurt Pastry Pasties

Alternatively, to make our simple yogurt pastry, mix 300g of plain white flour with a pinch of salt, 150g of natural yogurt and 3 tbsp of olive oil. Pour in 3-4 tbsp of cold water to help bring it all together. Roll out onto a floured surface. Cut into cereal bowl sized rounds. Dollop a spoonful of the cooked tagine mix in the centre of each round, leaving a 2cm rim. Brush the rim with a beaten egg. Lift and pull up the edges over the top of the filling in the centre. Pinch the edges together. Place on a baking sheet. Brush the outsides with the remaining egg. Bake in a preheated oven, at 180°C/Gas 4, for 25 mins or till golden.

Southern-Fried Cauli

In a region known in equal parts for its soul food and country music, we pay homage to America's Deep South with these cauliflower steaks. Make this simple recipe once and you'll never look at a cauli the same way again.

V | 10 MINS | 20 MINS | 2 AS A MAIN | 1

Southern fried-cauliflower:

1 large cauliflower

2 eggs

200g plain white or buckwheat flour (or a mix)

½ tsp sea salt

1 tbsp sweet smoked paprika

1 tsp ground cumin

100ml rapeseed or sunflower oil for frying

Freshly ground pepper

Buttermilk dressing:

100ml buttermilk or natural yogurt

3 tbsp mayonnaise

1 tsp Dijon mustard

A dash of Worcestershire sauce

A dash of hot chilli sauce (optional)

A handful of chives

Slice the cauliflower into thick steaks, about 2–3cm thick.

Place the cauliflower steaks in a large, lidded pan. Pour enough water to come halfway up the sides of the cauliflower. Bring to the boil. Lower the heat. Cover and simmer for 2–3 mins, or till the cauliflower is fork tender. Drain and let it cool completely.

Whisk the eggs in a shallow bowl. In a separate shallow bowl, mix the flour with the salt, spices and a generous pinch of pepper.

Dip both sides of the cooled cauliflower steaks in the flour mixture until coated completely. Toss the flour-coated cauliflower pieces in the eggs until they're evenly coated, then return to the flour mixture to toss again.

Set a large frying pan over a high heat. Add enough of the rapeseed or sunflower oil to the pan to create a 1cm-deep puddle. When the oil is hot, add the cauliflower steaks. Fry till golden on each side, then remove from the pan and sit on kitchen towels.

In a bowl, blend all the buttermilk dressing ingredients. Taste and add more Worcestershire or chilli sauce, as well as salt and pepper, if needed, to suit your palate. Drizzle the dressing over the warm cauliflower steaks.

Don't Touch that Compost Bin

Turn the leaves from your cauliflower into a gorgeous Cobb salad to serve alongside your cauli steaks. Wash the leaves well. Very finely chop. Toss with tomatoes, avocado, slices of red pepper, grated carrot (or whatever you've got to hand). Dress with more of the buttermilk dressing. If you eat meat, top with crunchy lardons of bacon.

AUTUMN

Apple Bobber's Guide

There are over 2,000 varieties of apples we could grow in the UK.

If you do nothing else this autumn, taste your way through as many of
the apple gems below that you can get your paws on.
Why not host a little apple tasting?

COLLINA

Collina apples are early growers but their season is short – once they are ready, they fall straight from the tree. A sweet flavour that is incredibly complex and delicious. Yellow-green with an orange-red striped blush.

DISCOVERY

Also known as 'Disco'. Wonderful crisp and juicy flesh with hints of pink due to its Beauty of Bath parentage. One of Britain's favourite apples, with good reason.

EGREMONT RUSSET

One of the oldest and most-loved Russets grown in England. They're green to light brown, with russetting on the skin. This doesn't affect the flavour – which is rich, sweet and nutty.

FALSTAFF

The apple of Shakespeare's eye, this gorgeous variety is stunning eaten straight from the fruit bowl. A Golden Delicious cross – yellow with blocks of red and very matt skin. Extremely juicy and sweet, with a hint of acidity.

FIESTA

A Cox-type apple. Crunchy, crisp and yellow, with blocks of light red and many stripes. They have a slightly tangy but fresh flavour.

GALAS

Mild and sweet in flavour, vertically striped or mottled, and a little orange in colour overall. Gala apples are sweet, fine textured and aromatic, making for a mighty fine apple sauce.

RED WINDSOR

A red version of the German 'Alkeme' variety, and sometimes known as Sweet Lilibet. Nothing to do with castles, but they are strong, tangy and juicy.

SATURN

Very smooth skin, which can vary from dark red to light. An organic-only breed, they're very sweet and juicy .

SPARTAN

Apples with a fantastic colour – almost dark purple. The longer you leave them in the fruit bowl, the sweeter they'll get. Kids love them.

West Country Quiche

Here's a quiche (and quick, we promise) history lesson: Quiche Lorraine actually has roots in what was once Germany, in the medieval kingdom of Lothringen, which later became the French region Lorraine. Ours has a considerable Dorset twang that makes it one for the history books in our opinion.

 20 MINS   45 MINS   6-8   ½

250g plain white flour

125g cold, unsalted butter

4 eggs

3½ tbsp cold water

100ml crème fraîche or double cream

1 onion, finely diced

200g Cheddar, grated

3 medium-sized eating apples, peeled and finely diced

100g smoked ham, shredded or diced

Freshly grated nutmeg

Sea salt and freshly ground pepper

Preheat your oven to 200°C/Gas 6.

Place the flour, butter and a pinch of salt in a bowl. Chop the butter into cubes, coating it in the flour as you go.

Separate one egg, adding the yolk to the mix and setting the white aside. Rub the butter and yolk through the flour till it's like fine breadcrumbs.

Sprinkle the water in, little by little, stirring. Work into a soft dough with your hands.

Roll the pastry out, 0.5–1cm thick, on a floured surface. You'll need a tart tin roughly 22cm in diameter – use it to check the pastry is big enough. Dust flour over the pastry. Gently fold in half, and again. Unfold in the tin and gently push it into the sides. Let it overhang a bit. Trim to fit. Line with baking paper. Fill with baking beans (or coins). Bake for 15 mins.

Whisk the remaining eggs and reserved egg white in a separate bowl. Whip in the crème fraîche or cream and a good crack of pepper. Mix in the onion, cheese, diced apple, ham and a little nutmeg.

When the pastry is crisp, remove the baking paper and beans/coins. Trim the pastry on the sides. Pour in the filling and smooth over. Bake for 30 mins or till golden and set.

Roast Toffee Apples

A super quick and easy caramel sauce means that you can start tucking into meltingly tender seasonal apples all the more sharpish.

 15 MINS 25 MINS 8-12 1

8-12 medium-sized apples

100g Demerara or brown sugar

100g unsalted butter, cubed

125g single cream

Sea salt

Ice cream, cream, crème fraîche or custard, to serve

Preheat your oven to 180°C/Gas 4.

Remove the cores from your apples with a small knife or corer. Cut a 1cm-deep slice around the circumference of each apple. This gives them room to swell without bursting their skins.

Line a 12-hole muffin tin with squares of baking paper or muffin liners. Set an apple in each one. Bake at the top of the oven for 20-25 mins, or till fully tender. The amount of time really depends on the variety of apple you use, so just keep an eye on it.

Set a saucepan over a medium-high heat. Add the sugar and cook, stirring, till it's fully dissolved. Whisk in the butter, cream and a pinch of salt. Gently simmer till everything is melted and silky.

Pour the toffee into the centre of the roasted apples. Serve on their own or with ice cream (or any cream or crème fraîche or custard). Also stunning if set on top of a warm piece of parkin or ginger cake.

Mash It Up

Take the tuber challenge! See if you can try as many potato varieties as possible over the next 12 months. There's such a rainbow of colours, flavours and textures to be discovered. These are a few of our faves.

ANYA
Long, finger-shaped tubers with a firm waxy texture and a pleasant, slightly nutty flavour.

ARRAN VICTORY
Vivid rosy skin with contrasting white flesh, which is floury and very tasty.

ATHLETE
A new variety of potato developed for the 2012 Olympics. Tasty, pale yellow flesh. Remain firm when boiled, and are great hot or cold in salads.

BAMBINO
Small round white tubers with light cream flesh and a superb taste. Less waxy than other salad potatoes, so don't over-boil.

ESTIMA
Firm, light yellow flesh with earthy flavour notes. Holds its shape when cooked. These spuds have a smooth, velvety texture so they're ideal for recipes like Dauphinoise, soups or mash.

MILVA
With flavour to rival the salad varieties, these attractive potatoes are long and oval, with a waxy yellow flesh and good flavour. Delicious both hot and cold.

ORLA
Very tasty white tubers with yellow flesh and skin, and a waxier texture than traditional varieties.

RUDOLPH
Delicious white flesh and vibrant red skin. Makes the most incredible roasties and chips. Also makes for a stunning jacket or smooth, creamy mash.

Hazelnut & Thyme's Greatest Gratin

'Boil 'em, mash 'em, stick 'em in a stew.' He may have been wise, but he left 'gratin' off the list. These versatile tubers are the beloved food of hobbits and humans alike.

 **V** | 10 MINS | 1 HR 15 MINS | 6 | 1

2 garlic cloves, thinly sliced

A large handful of thyme sprigs

1 lemon, zest only

200ml white wine

220ml double cream

400g potatoes

3 fennel bulbs

50g Parmesan or vegetarian equivalent

75g hazelnuts

Sea salt and freshly ground pepper

Preheat your oven to 200°C/Gas 6.

Scrape the garlic into a pan with the thyme sprigs, lemon zest, white wine and cream. Bring to the boil, then lower the heat and simmer for 10 mins.

Slice the potatoes (leave the skin on if you like, or peel if you prefer) and fennel as thinly as possible (use a mandolin if you have one). Tumble into a baking dish.

Pour the infused cream over the potatoes. Toss together. Season with a pinch of salt and pepper.

Cover the dish with foil or a lid. Bake for 50 mins. Remove the foil. The veg should be tender and the cream thickened. Grate the cheese over the top and scatter with the hazelnuts.

Return to the oven for 15 mins to brown the top.

Gazza's Indian Hotpot

Gaz, our fabulous photographer in residence, has many strings to his bow. Cooking is another and this is one of his creations: a perfectly speedy, one-pan supper.

 10 MINS 45 MINS 4

4 lamb chops

1 tbsp mild curry powder

1 large onion, thinly sliced

175ml water

2 good-sized spuds or 4-5 smaller ones, peeled and thinly sliced

1 tbsp olive oil

Sea salt and freshly ground pepper

A handful of fresh parsley (optional), to serve

Preheat your oven to 200°C/Gas 6.

Put your chops in a snug baking dish. Dust the curry powder over. Massage the curry powder into the meat, rubbing it in all over.

Scatter the onion over the top of your lamb. Pour in the water.

Give your spuds a rinse to remove some of their starch. In a bowl, toss with the olive oil and a nice twist of salt and pepper.

Arrange the potato slices over the onion-topped lamb. You want the slices to overlap slightly, creating a nice cobbled topping.

Cover the whole dish tightly with foil. Bake for 30 mins. Remove the foil. Cook for a further 15 mins, or till the spuds have a nice golden crust.

Lovely served with a scattering of chopped parsley over the top. Delicious with a crisp green salad and a dollop of natural yogurt mixed with a handful of finely chopped fresh mint.

Winter Waldorf Soup

We've taken all the flavours from the classic Waldorf salad and turned the heat up. The result? A rich, earthy and warming soup ready for crusty bread dunking.

 V 🥄 15 MINS 🍲 30-35 MINS 🍴 4 ❤ 1

2 tbsp olive oil

1 white onion, finely chopped

2 potatoes, peeled and finely chopped

2 celery sticks, finely sliced

2 bay leaves

2 apples

2 veg stock cubes in 1.5 ltr boiling water or 1.5 ltr homemade stock

75g walnut halves

Sea salt and freshly ground pepper

Warm a pan over a low heat for 1 min. Add the oil and the onion. Season. Fry for 8 mins, stirring now and then.

Add the potato and celery to the pan with the bay leaves. Season. Fry for 5 mins, stirring now and then.

Peel and quarter the apples. Slice out the apple cores. Roughly chop. Crumble the stock cube into a heatproof jug, add the boiling water and stir. Add the apple and stock to the pan. Cover and bring to the boil. Simmer for 15-20 mins till the veg are very soft.

Tip the walnuts into a dry frying pan. Toast over a medium heat, shaking the pan, for 2-3 mins. Tip onto a board. Leave to cool, then roughly chop.

Remove the bay leaves. Ladle the soup into a blender and blitz until smooth, or use a handheld blender in the pan. Taste and season. Serve topped with the walnuts.

Swede & Coconut Daal

This Anglicised daal is cosier than a pair of woolly slippers and tastes miles better, too. It makes a wonderful bed for whole roasted pheasant, or keep it veggie and serve with rice, fried onions and naan bread.

 (WITH MEAT OPTION!)   15 MINS   45 MINS   4   1

A gloss of olive or coconut oil

210g finely diced swede, carrot or squash

2 bay leaves

1 whole red chilli

1 cinnamon stick

280g red lentils or yellow split peas, rinsed

1 onion, finely diced, or 6 garlic cloves, chopped

1 tbsp freshly grated ginger

2 tsp cumin seeds

1 tsp ground coriander

350ml coconut milk

1 litre water

1 lime or lemon, zest and juice

A handful of dessicated coconut and/or almonds, toasted

A large handful of fresh coriander

Sea salt and freshly ground pepper

Gloss a large hot pan with a little oil. Add your diced swede, carrot or squash. Season. Sizzle till just softened and starting to colour a bit.

Add the bay leaves, chilli and cinnamon stick. Swirl in the lentils, onion or garlic, ginger, cumin and coriander. Pour in the coconut milk and water. Pop a lid on. Simmer for 45 mins or till all the liquid is absorbed into the lentils. Give it a good stir every 10 mins or so. Trickle in a little more water as and when needed.

Taste. Whip in more spices if you like. Season with salt and pepper.

Finish with a hit of lime or lemon zest and a squeeze of juice, toasted coconut and/or almonds, and fresh coriander.

For the Pheasant to Perch on Top

For four people, you will need one or two pheasants, depending on size. Preheat your oven to 200°C/Gas 6. Unwrap your birds to let them warm up to room temperature. Season the pheasants all over. Add a nugget of butter and a splash of olive oil to a large frying pan over a medium-high heat. Brown the pheasants all over. Pop them in the oven. The pheasants will need about 30 mins, depending on size. If you've got quite a plump bird that looks more like a small chicken, add another 5-10 mins. It will be done when you can pull the leg away from the breast with ease and there is no sign of pinky/red flesh when you do.

Rumbledethumps

Our recipe guru Rachel de Thample (which makes this Racheldethamp's Rumbeldethumps) loves this greeny rooty Scottish dish. You'll love this one because it works with any root veg you might have lying about.

V | 10 MINS | 45 MINS | 4 | 1

1kg spuds and/or root veg, peeled and cubed (see tip)

3 garlic cloves, crushed

A knob of butter

A splash of warm milk

A gloss of olive oil

½ green cabbage or 3 large handfuls of kale, tough stalks removed and finely shredded

1 small onion, finely chopped

150g Cheddar (or similar), grated

A couple of thyme sprigs, leaves only

Sea salt and freshly ground pepper

Preheat your oven to 200°C/Gas 6.

Tumble your spuds/roots into a large pot. Cover with water. Add a good pinch of salt and the garlic.

Bring to the boil. Cook till the spuds and roots are mashably tender. Drain. Mash with the butter and milk. Season to taste.

Get a large frying pan hot. Add a gloss of olive oil and the cabbage or kale and onion. Sizzle till tender and glossy. Season well. Remove from the heat while the cabbage is still bright green. Stir through the mash.

Pop the cabbage/mash medley into a baking dish. Scatter with the cheese. Bake till the cheese is golden, about 25 mins. Finish with the fresh thyme.

Serve as a vegetarian main alongside a salad, or dish up as a side to a casserole or Sunday roast.

Back to Your Roots

We used a 50/50 mix of potatoes and swede. You can use just roots, or swap the swede for parsnips, celeriac or turnips.

Boogie On Down to Earth

Ninety-five per cent of the world's food relies on soil. Sounds obvious, but it needs to be healthy for all the food growing in it to be sustainable.

In just one handful of organic soil there are more living organisms than people on the planet. Now that's a party.

Literally billions of healthy bacteria go about their daily business supporting the plants that grow around them.

Non-organic farming practices can weaken the top soil so it simply blows away. Naturally resilient soil can stand up to a bit of weather.

Organic farmers follow a crop rotation that keeps the soil fertile and prevents a build-up of pests, weeds and diseases. Nitrogen is added naturally by growing clover and spreading composted manure and seaweed on their fields.

Soil also brings flavour to the hoe-down. Our leeks from James Brown (soil singer, not soul singer) actually taste leekier because of naturally higher levels of sulphur in his rich, organic soil.

Cardamom, Walnut & Pear Chicken

The Abel & Cole kitchen was buzzing when we sounded the dinner bell for this dish. Simple and peared back, yet a stunner of a roast. Dish it out with a good helping of celeriac couscous (over on page 219).

 20 MINS   40 MINS   6   1

6 chicken legs

Seeds from 6 cardamom pods

1 lemon, zest and squeeze of juice

6 garlic cloves

4 large or 6 smaller pears

4 tbsp water

2 rosemary sprigs, leaves only, finely chopped

A large handful of walnuts

2 tbsp honey

Sea salt and freshly ground pepper

Preheat your oven to 200°C/Gas 6.

Put your chicken in a large roasting dish. Grind the seeds from your cardamom pods into a coarse powder. Dust this over the chicken, along with the lemon zest and a good pinch of salt and pepper.

Flatten each clove of garlic with the side of a knife. Whip off the skin. Tuck a clove under each piece of chicken.

Peel and quarter your pears. Cut the cores out and trim off the stems. Juice your lemon. In a bowl, toss with your pears, then tuck the pears in the dish with the chicken.

Roast the chicken on the top shelf of your oven for 30 mins or till golden and the juices run clear when you prick the fattest part of the leg with the tip of a knife. Cook a little longer, if needed.

Add the water to the dish. Scatter the rosemary over the chicken, along with the walnuts. Drizzle the honey over the top. Finish with a dusting of salt and pepper. Pop back in the oven for 5 mins, or till the walnuts are golden.

Haunch of Venison with Rosemary & Pear Stuffing

Wild venison is wonderfully lean. Wrap it in bacon and stuff it with honeyed, lemony, rosemary-flecked pears and you'll have a wonderfully sweet and succulent roast. This is stunning served with parsnip mash and a side of blanched kale tossed with toasted almonds.

 15 MINS 30 MINS 8-10 ½

1.5kg haunch of venison
1 garlic bulb
2 rosemary sprigs, leaves only
1 lemon, zest
2 tbsp honey
6 pears
250g smoked streaky bacon
250ml perry or cider
Sea salt and freshly ground pepper

Preheat your oven to 220°C/Gas 7.

Strip off all the wrapping (and the net) from your venison. Find a spot down the centre where it has a natural opening or seam. Run your knife along it to open it out, so you have room to stuff it.

Finely chop two garlic cloves. Finely chop the rosemary leaves and lemon zest. In a bowl, mix the garlic, rosemary and lemon zest with 1 tbsp of the honey and a pinch of salt and pepper. Rub the mixture over the venison.

Peel and quarter your pears. Trim out the cores and stems. Thinly slice six of the pear quarters. Tuck these into the cut you've made in the venison, right down the middle. Roll the venison to secure the stuffing in the centre. Wrap the streaky bacon around the joint, working from one end to the other to hold it together. Use toothpicks or butcher's string to secure it.

Set the venison in a roasting tin. Arrange the remaining pear quarters around the meat. Halve the remaining garlic bulb and tuck the halves under the meat. Roast on the top shelf of the oven for 30 mins or till the bacon is golden and crisp.

Remove the meat from the tin to rest. Pluck out the pear quarters and arrange around the meat. Strain the juices into a saucepan, pressing on the garlic halves to extract some of their flavour. Set it over a high heat. Add half the perry or cider. Simmer until it has reduced by about half. Swirl in 1 tbsp of honey. Taste. Add a little water or more perry to taste. Strain into a jug and serve alongside the carved meat and roasted pears.

Honeybear Pear Flapjacks

Like your flapjacks extra sticky? Pear and honey will do just the trick.
Not a pear to spare? Swap for the same weight of grated apple or a
mashed-up banana.

 V 15 MINS 30 MINS 12 1

100g unsalted butter (see tip)

100g brown sugar

75g honey

1 tsp vanilla extract or seeds
from ½ vanilla pod

1 lemon, zest only (optional)

200g porridge oats

1 tsp mixed spice

200g nuts (whole or chopped)
and/or seeds

150g coarsely grated pear

Sea salt

Preheat your oven to 160°C/Gas 3. Line a 20cm square tin (or
something of a similar size) with baking paper. It makes getting the
flapjacks out much easier.

Melt the butter, sugar, honey, vanilla and lemon zest (if using) in
a saucepan on a low heat, till the sugar dissolves.

Mix the oats, mixed spice, the nuts and/or seeds together, with
a good pinch of sea salt. Fold the grated pear through.

Stir the melted butter mix through the oat mix till it is sticky and
thick.

Press the mix into your prepared tin. Bake in the centre of the
middle shelf for 30 mins or till the flapjacks are golden on the top
and crispy around the edges.

For best results, allow to cool fully before cutting into them: tricky,
but worth the wait.

This Way, Vegans

Use coconut oil instead of the
butter, and maple syrup or
agave syrup in place of the
honey. It'll give the flapjacks a
softer consistency but they're
still delicious nonetheless.

No-Knead Slow Fermentation Bread

Making your own bread might seem a bit daunting at first, especially if you've never tried it before. Master this loaf, which is as easy as lacing your shoes, and you'll have fantastic home-baked bread on tap for the rest of your life. It's been the go-to bread recipe for Abel & Colers for years.

 15 MINS, PLUS 14 HRS PROVING   35-45 MINS   1 LARGE LOAF

400g strong white flour, plus extra for dusting

½ tsp instant yeast

1 tsp sea salt

350ml lukewarm water

1 tbsp good olive oil

In a large bowl, combine flour, yeast and salt. Add the lukewarm water and olive oil. Give it a quick stir with your hands or a plastic spatula. The dough will be a little loose and sticky. Cover the bowl with cling film and let the dough rest for about 12 hrs at warm room temperature. The dough should double in size and be covered in small bubbles.

Scrape the dough out of the bowl with a plastic spatula and onto a lightly floured work surface. Sprinkle with a little more flour and fold it over on itself two or three times. Turn it over seam-side down and shape into a ball. Try not to overwork the dough, and use a little more flour to stop it from sticking if need be.

Put the dough ball into a lightly oiled, round heatproof dish/pot/tin (about 25cm in diameter). Cover with a tea towel and let it rest for 1-2 hrs till it rises again.

Preheat your oven to 200°C/Gas 6.

Pop the tin into the oven and bake for about 35–45 mins till the bread has a good crust and makes a hollow sound when tapped on its bottom. Turn it out onto a rack to cool for at least 20 mins (if you can last that long) before tucking in.

A Loaf of Good Intention

Making your own bread is not only deeply relaxing – a brilliant break away from your phone – it can be a relief to your digestive system too. Simple, natural ingredients along with a slower fermentation process, makes it easier for your body to digest. Thus, making this loaf is like bread yoga for your mind and your gut.

Late Summer Tricolore Salad

Professor Plum himself would get to the bottom of this dish before solving any would-be mysteries. Balsamic roasted plums, crispy rosemary and fennel seeds are the clues here. Opt for deliciously sweet Victoria plums if you can, although any plum will do.

 V · 15 MINS · 20 MINS · 4 · 1½

8 biggish or 12 smallish plums

4 tbsp balsamic vinegar

4 rosemary sprigs

1 orange, zest and 3 tbsp juice

3 tbsp olive oil, plus a drizzle for frying

100g rocket

2 balls of mozzarella (see tip)

½ chilli, thinly sliced

1 tsp fennel seeds (optional)

Sea salt and freshly ground pepper

Preheat your oven to 200°C/Gas 6.

Halve and stone your plums. Arrange them in an ovenproof dish. Add the balsamic vinegar and two of the rosemary sprigs. Roast for 15–20 mins till sticky, sweet and tender.

Zest your orange into a bowl. Mix with 3 tbsp of freshly squeezed orange juice and the olive oil. Whisk until fully mixed. Toss the rocket in the dressing.

Arrange the rocket on plates or a big platter. Tear your mozzarella into nuggets. Dot the nuggets of creamy mozzarella and sticky plum halves over the top of the salad.

Strip the rosemary leaves from the remaining sprigs. Roughly chop. Set a frying pan over a high heat. Add a drizzle of oil. Fry the rosemary, chilli and fennel seeds (if using) with a pinch of salt, till just crisp and fragrant.

Spoon the mixture and any residual oil over the top of the salad. Finish with a little dusting of pepper.

Veggie Cheese, Please

Instead of mozzarella, use 150g of soft goats' or ewes' milk cheese for a vegetarian option.

Plum & Bay Custard Tart

While organic plums and bay leaves wouldn't seem like such a gorgeous match on paper, we truly ate our words (and this pud) once our Jassy served it up.

 V 45 MINS, PLUS 30 MINS INFUSING 1 HR 30 MINS 6-8 1

For the pastry:
185g plain flour, plus extra for dusting

75g caster sugar

115g cold butter

1 egg

1 tbsp cold water

Sea salt

For the custard:
125ml whole milk

125ml double cream

½ vanilla pod

A handful of bay leaves

3 egg yolks

40g caster sugar

1 tsp plain flour

5 or 6 plums

For the sauce:
5 or 6 plums

25g caster sugar

Icing sugar, to dust

Freshly ground pepper

First, make the pastry. Sift the flour into a bowl with the caster sugar and a pinch of salt. Add the butter and rub it in with your fingertips to make fine crumbs.

In a bowl, whisk the egg with the cold water. Set 1 tbsp of the mixture aside to use as an egg wash later. Add the rest to the flour, 1 tbsp at a time, and gently stir with your hand till the pastry comes together. Wrap the pastry in cling film and chill for 1 hr.

Meanwhile, make the custard. Pour the milk and cream into a pan. Scrape the vanilla seeds out of the pod into the pan, then chuck in the pod. Add the bay leaves.

Bring the milk to the boil, stirring now and then. Take the milk off the heat and leave to infuse for 30 mins. Strain the infused milk. Gently reheat so it's steaming hot but not boiling.

In a bowl, whisk the egg yolks, caster sugar and flour together. Slowly whisk in the hot milk, a little at a time, till you have a thick, smooth custard.

Preheat your oven to 180°C/Gas 4.

Carefully roll out the pastry on a lightly floured surface. Line a 23cm round tart tin – the pastry will be quite soft. Add more flour if it's too soft to work with. Chill for 30 mins.

Line the pastry with baking paper and fill with baking beans or rice. Bake for 20 mins or till the pastry feels firm. Take out the paper and beans. Brush the pastry with the saved egg wash. Bake for another 15 mins till pale golden.

Turn the oven down to 160°C/Gas 3. Quarter five or six plums and scoop out the stones. Arrange the plums in the pastry case. Pour in the custard and bake for 30-40 mins till the tart is just set but wobbles a little when shaken. Leave to cool.

Halve, stone and roughly chop the plums for the sauce. Pop them in a pan with the caster sugar and plenty of black pepper. Cook and stir for 10 mins till they break down and make a thick sauce. Press through a sieve so you have a thin, clear sauce. Serve slices of the tart with the sauce, decorated with some bay leaves and a dusting of icing sugar.

Sugar Plums

'Tis the season to jeté for joy for British plums. This sweet, sugar-coated treat is, of course, inspired by the classic ballet, *The Nutcracker*, based on the book by E.T.A. Hoffmann.

 V 15 MINS 15 MINS 4 1

1 egg white

100g caster sugar

1 tsp ground cinnamon

8 cloves, ground

8 plums

250g mascarpone

A drizzle of wildflower honey

Preheat your oven to 200°C/Gas 6.

Whisk the egg white in a bowl. Stir in your sugar and half the cinnamon and ground cloves.

Dip the plums into the mix, turning to coat thoroughly.

Place the plums in a buttered baking dish. Roast in the oven for 10–15 mins or till crisp and golden brown.

While the plums cook, put your mascarpone in a bowl with a good drizzle of honey.

Serve the plums with the honey mascarpone and a dusting of the remaining spices.

You Simply Must Meringue

The egg white leaves a brilliant meringue-like crust in the baking dish. You can scrape it off and scatter it over the mascarpone cream. It's the new 'licking the bowl'!

Chocolate Cloud Biscuits

If ever a biscuit recipe was worthy of a love letter, this would be the one – melt-in-your-mouth, deliciously light pillows of chocolate with their subtle hints of winter citrus and spice. The only problem is, one bite and you'll be lost for words.

 V 15 MINS 10 MINS 12

50g unsalted butter

250g dark chocolate, chopped

2 eggs

A hint of spice (see tip)

150g brown sugar

2 oranges or clementines, zest and 4 tbsp juice, plus extra zest to decorate

50g white plain flour

½ tsp baking powder

Sea salt

Preheat your oven to 180°C/Gas 4.

Put the butter and 200g of the chocolate in a heatproof bowl over a saucepan of simmering water (do not let the bowl touch the water) until the chocolate is melted. Roughly chop the remaining chocolate. Set both aside.

Separate the egg yolks and whites into separate bowls. Whisk the whites with a pinch of salt till you have light, fluffy and meringue-like stiff peaks.

In a bowl, whisk the yolks, spice, sugar, orange zest and juice with an electric mixer or handheld electric whisk till the mixture lightens, about 5 mins. Spoon the melted chocolate into the yolk mix. Whisk till smooth and glossy.

Fold the egg whites through the mix, little by little, till fully mixed through. Sift in the flour and baking powder, little by little, again till mixed through. Fold through the chopped chocolate. The mix will be a bit runny but should hold its shape once dolloped onto the tray. If not, just sift in and fold through an extra 50g of flour.

Dollop rounded tablespoons of the mixture onto a baking paper-lined baking tray, leaving space between each dollop. Cook in batches, if needed. Bake for 10 mins, or till the biscuits are set and a little cracked on top.

Leave to cool before removing from the tray. Lovely finished with a little pinch of sea salt and orange zest on top.

Spice Things Up

Whisk a scraping of vanilla seeds or extract, ground cinnamon, a pinch of chilli powder and/or ground cardamom in with the egg yolks to give a hint of spice to your biccies.

Goodness Gracious Greens

We're mad about smoothies and prefer them to
juicing as you get bundles of fibre added to the mix as well
as heaps of fruit and veg portions with just a few delicious sips.
Here are two of our favourite green smoothies to give you
an autumnal immunity boost.

Matcha of the Day

Matcha is made from whole green leaves that are dried and ground into a
powder, giving you a serious antioxidant boost.

 5 MINS 0 2 2

1 avocado

2 bananas

2 tsp matcha powder

400ml almond milk or
coconut water

Ensure your avocado is ripe before you blend. We like to put them
a bag with our bananas to help them ripen. When your avocado is
ripe and ready, peel it with a sharp knife and remove the stone.
Peel the bananas. Blend everything together until smooth. Whizz
a little water in to thin, if needed.

Popeye Pears

Out of spinach? Just use kale, watercress, chard or rocket.

 5 MINS 0 2

4 ripe pears

100g baby leaf spinach

250ml water or milk

1 lemon, zest and juice

Roughly chop the pears, discarding the stems and cores (keep the
skin on for ultimate goodness, or peel if you prefer a smoother
finish). Blend with the spinach, the water or milk (add more, if
needed) and enough lemon zest and juice to tickle your taste buds.

Pear & Rosemary G&T

Gin-lover Jassy has come up with the perfect autumnal gin and tonic, flavoured with seasonal pears and aromatic rosemary. Next time you throw a get-together impress your guests with this amazing little drink.

 15 MINS, PLUS 1 HR INFUSING 5-8 MINS 6

2 pears

100g caster sugar

125ml cold water

A few rosemary sprigs

A squeeze of lemon juice

Ice

180ml Juniper Green Dry London Gin

Tonic water

Core one of the pears for the syrup and roughly chop it. Pop it in a pan with the sugar, water and one large rosemary sprig. Cover and cook over a medium heat, stirring now and then, for 5–8 mins till the pear has broken down and is really soft. Take off the heat and leave for 1 hr to infuse.

Strain the liquid through a sieve into a bowl, pressing down to squeeze as much juice as possible out of the pear. For a really smooth syrup, you can strain the syrup for a second time, lining the sieve with muslin to catch any pulp, but it's not essential. Chill till needed.

To assemble the G&Ts, thinly slice the other pear (on a mandolin, if you have one), and toss with a little lemon juice. Fill glasses with ice. Pour 30ml of gin into each glass. Top up with tonic water. Add 1–2 tsp of syrup to each glass and stir to mix the gin, tonic and syrup. Slide in a slice or two of pear and a sprig of rosemary (stripping the leaves from the bottom half of the sprig). Serve straight away.

Extra, Extra!

You'll have leftover syrup. It will keep in the fridge for around a week, or you can freeze little shots of it in ice cube trays, ready for adding to your G&Ts in the future. It's great by itself with soda water, or drizzle over yogurt and serve with chopped fruit.

Crab Apple Whisky

Tart little crab apples are ripe for picking from September, and they don't stick around for long. Nab a bundle to make this gorgeous tipple, which will be ready just in time for Christmas.

 15 MINS 0 10-12

About 750g crab apples

70cl whisky

5 tbsp honey or sugar

3 slices of fresh ginger

Give your crab apples a good wash and dry. Halve. Place in a 1-litre sterilised jar (page 114). Top up the jar with whisky as you go. Swirl in the honey or sugar. Tuck in your ginger slices or any other spices you might want to add (a cinnamon stick, halved vanilla pod, cardamom, cloves).

Make sure the apples are fully covered by the whisky. Secure the lid. Let it infuse till Christmas, or longer if you can wait. If you can, leave it for up to 3-5 years - it'll veer towards the likes of Calvados. So, maybe make one for now, and one for later.

Mexican Popping Sweetcorn

The fastest way to eat sweetcorn is to cut the raw kernels off the cob. Get a frying pan super-hot, add a little oil or butter and fry the kernels till golden and popping in the pan. Sprinkle some cumin seeds and chilli flakes in the pan for a Mexican vibe. Finish with a hint of lime juice and zest. Lovely in tacos with fried halloumi, red peppers, avocado and coriander.

Plummy Pork Chops

Cut the fatty rind off a pork chop and cook it (the rind) in a smoking hot frying pan till crisp and crackly. Salt it well. Add your pork to the pan with some fennel seeds and halved plums. Cook for 3 mins or till golden on each side. Drizzle a little honey over. Flash-cook in the oven on 200°C/ Gas 6 for 10 mins to finish cooking through. Voilà! Serve with rocket and a drizzle of balsamic.

Lemon & Pear Sorbet

Peel, core, dice and freeze your ripe pears with a squeeze of lemon juice. Once frozen, you can whizz them up into an instant sorbet in a food processor with a little icing sugar or a cold drop of dessert wine. Lovely with a hint of mixed spice.

Pumpkin & Chorizo Hash

Coarsely grate a pumpkin or squash (skin on if thin). Set a large frying pan over a high heat. Add a coating of oil. Add the pumpkin or squash in a fairly thin (2–3cm) layer. Add 2 finely chopped garlic cloves. Season well. Fry till tender and golden around the edges. Crumble in nuggets of chorizo and cumin seeds towards the end of cooking. Finish with chopped parsley or crispy sage leaves. Delicious with a fried egg or pan-fried hake.

Ginger Wok Cauliflower

Set a wok or large frying pan over a high heat. Finely chop your cauliflower and the smaller, softer outer leaves, too. Add to the wok with a tbsp of coconut oil and a pinch of salt. Sizzle till just golden. Toss in a 3cm piece of fresh ginger (cut into thin matchsticks), 1 or 2 thinly sliced garlic cloves, a sprinkle of sesame seeds and fresh chilli (if you like). Finish with a slosh of tamari or soy sauce and a squeeze of orange juice. Delicious with rice.

Swedish Roast Swede

Cut your peeled swede into smallish cubes. Toss with oil, salt and pepper. Tumble onto a large roasting tray preheated in a 200°C/Gas 6 oven. Roast for 20 mins or till tender and a little crisp on the outside – or pan-fry in oil. Serve with dollops of crème fraîche mixed with fresh dill or caraway seeds.

WINTER

Log fires and rosy cheeks,
winter's for good food and good times.
Feast on roasts, bejewelled puds with pomegranate,
and peel the first blood orange of the season with glee.
Oh, and mull everything in sight.

Seasonal Stars
Parsnip, kale, swede, dates, celeriac, sprouts,
citrus, beetroot, leeks, pomegranate

Carbon Sinks

A good lot of our organic parsnips come from Bagthorpe Farm, in the beautiful unspoilt countryside of rural North Norfolk, near the Sandringham estate, which is surrounded by a vast 150-acre swathe of woodland.

Donald Morton, who runs the family farm, says it's a haven for rare bats. The wooded areas are dense with ancient oaks, beech and ash trees, as well as chestnuts and sycamores. In combination, the woodland, and the farm's organic status, act as a carbon sink, which effectively means the farm absorbs more carbon than it releases as carbon dioxide.

'We undertook a Carbon Footprint audit and discovered that our total emissions of CO_2 (including the methane and nitrous oxide equivalent tonnage) was 307 tonnes annually,' beams Donald, 'whereas thanks to our farming practices (reduction of artificial fertilisers on the organically farmed area) and the woodland we actually sequester 669 tonnes of CO_2 annually, meaning we are in credit!

Parsnip & Blue Cheese Gratin

The weather outside may be frightful yet this meltingly creamy parsnip gratin is more than delightful. Wonderful at any point in the season, the tangy blue cheese gives this dish plenty of intrigue, and it's a winner if there's any leftover Christmas cheese (is there such a thing?). It's a good veggie main – worthy even of Christmas Day.

 V · 20 MINS · 30 MINS · 2-4 · 1

4 large parsnips, peeled and chopped into 2cm cubes

4 large potatoes, peeled and chopped into 2cm cubes

500ml full-cream milk

1 bay leaf

100g blue cheese

A handful of thyme, leaves only

Sea salt and freshly ground pepper

Place the parsnips and potatoes in a pan. Pour in the milk. Drop in the bay leaf. Bring to a simmer over a medium heat, then turn the heat down and simmer for 10 mins till the veg is just tender when pierced with a sharp knife.

Heat your grill to medium high. No grill? Set your oven to its highest temperature. When the veg is tender, use a slotted spoon to lift it out of the pan (keeping the milk) and pop it into a baking dish. Discard the bay leaf. Crumble the blue cheese into the dish. Add the thyme leaves, a pinch of salt and a good crack of black pepper. Lightly mash it all together with 2–3 tbsp of the warm milk. It should be slightly loose.

Slide the gratin under the grill for 5 mins till it's golden and bubbling. Delicious served with garlicky greens or a simple watercress and apple salad.

Parsnip & Mushroom Pan Pie

Few things are cosier than a proper homemade pie. We often wonder why creamy, sweet and rooty parsnips aren't more popular. They make for a stunner of a meat-free main paired with some 'shrooms.

 V · 15 MINS · 45 MINS · 4 · 1

2 tbsp dried porcini mushrooms

125ml boiling water

3 tbsp olive oil

1 large onion, thinly sliced

600g chestnut mushrooms, thinly sliced

2 garlic cloves, finely chopped

250g crème fraîche

1 tbsp Dijon mustard

3 large parsnips or potatoes, peeled and coarsely grated

2 rosemary sprigs, leaves only, finely chopped

1 lemon, zest only

Sea salt and freshly ground pepper

Preheat your oven to 200°C/Gas 6. Pop your porcini into a small heatproof bowl and cover with the boiling water. Leave to soak for 10 mins.

Heat 1 tbsp of olive oil in an ovenproof frying pan (see tip) over a medium-high heat. Add the onion and lower the heat. Cook for 5 mins or till tender and glossy.

Add the mushrooms to the onion. Season. Cook over a medium-high heat for around 5 mins or till the moisture has cooked out of the mushrooms. Add the garlic for the last 1 min.

Add the porcini and their soaking liquid to the pan. Cook and stir for 1–2 mins. Take off the heat. Stir the crème fraîche and mustard through. Season to taste.

Place your grated parsnips into a large bowl with the rosemary and lemon zest. Season. Pour in 2 tbsp of olive oil. Scatter the mix over the mushrooms. Pop into the oven on a high shelf. Bake for 30 mins or till the parsnips are golden and crisp. Delicious with a side of garlicky kale or a watercress and preserved lemon salad.

Out of the Frying Pan

If your frying pan isn't ovenproof, tumble the creamy mushroom mix into a small baking dish. Cover with the grated parsnips and cook as above.

Golden Maple & Walnut Parsnips

If you go into the woods today you'll fancy something to eat about lunchtime.
This dish takes its cue from the forest. It's nutty, sweet and full of adventure.

 V · 15 MINS · 45 MINS · 4 · 1

1-2 tbsp rapeseed oil

700g parsnips, peeled

4 rosemary sprigs

2 clementines, halved

A large handful of walnuts

2 tbsp maple syrup

Sea salt and freshly ground
pepper

Preheat your oven to 220°C/Gas 7. Half-fill a large pan with cold water. Add a pinch of salt. Pour the rapeseed oil into a roasting tin, enough to create a 1cm layer in the pan. Pop the tin in the oven to heat through.

Slice the parsnips into long lengths about 2.5cm wide. Add them to the pan of cold water. Pop on a lid. Bring to the boil. Boil till just tender, about 5 mins. Drain.

Tip the parsnips into the roasting tin with the rosemary sprigs, halved clementines and a good pinch of salt and pepper. Shake the pan a few times to coat the veg in the oil. Roast for 30-35 mins till golden and crisp.

Once golden, fold in the walnuts and maple syrup. Roast for a further 5 mins. This is delicious as a festive side, or toss with leaves and/or grains to turn into a hearty winter salad. You can also puree leftovers with stock and a splash of cream for an instant soup.

Flower Power Sprouts with Anchovy Dressing

While they may not have as much international fame as The Rockettes, Kalettes® (also known as Flower Sprouts) are in a class all of their own. They're a cross between Brussels sprouts and kale and you'll thank your lucky greens you've discovered them. A doddle to cook, they taste smashing dressed with a punchy mix of anchovy and mustard.

 10 MINS   2 MINS   4   1

400g flower sprouts

1 large garlic clove, crushed

4 anchovy fillets, drained and finely chopped

2 tsp Dijon mustard

1 lemon, zest and juice

2 tbsp olive oil

Sea salt and freshly ground pepper

Bring a large pan of salted water to the boil. Give the sprouts a good rinse and trim the very dry ends off without separating the leaves.

When the water is boiling, add the sprouts. Simmer for 2 mins. Drain and rinse under cold water to stop them cooking. Leave them in the colander while you make the dressing.

Pop the crushed garlic in a bowl. Add the anchovy fillets and Dijon mustard to the bowl. Grate in the lemon zest and squeeze in the juice from the lemon.

Add the oil with a little pinch of salt and plenty of pepper. Whisk together with a fork to make a chunky dressing. Taste and add more salt or lemon juice if you think the dressing needs it.

Tip the sprouts into a bowl. Add the dressing. Toss to coat. Serve straight away.

Dickensian Gammon

You're in for a treat, Bumble. This 'ere roast is inspired by one of Charles Dickens' favourite Victorian dishes, Fidget Pie: a medley of gammon, apples, potatoes, sugar, spice and sage. To serve eight people, double the recipe and increase both the boiling and the roasting time by 30 mins.

20 MINS, PLUS OVERNIGHT SOAKING (OR 1 HR BOILING)   1 HOUR 45 MINS   4   1

1.2kg gammon joint

1 tbsp mixed spice

3 apples

500g potatoes, peeled and thinly sliced

1 onion, thinly sliced

A handful of sage, leaves only

1 tbsp Demerara sugar

Unwrap your gammon. Strip off the netting. Pop into a large pot. Cover with water. Pop in the fridge and soak overnight. No time for overnight soaking? Just boil in water for 1 hr for a quick fix. This step removes excess saltiness.

Drain the soaked or par-boiled gammon and pop it in a clean pan. Dust all of the mixed spice over it. Cover with water. Pop on the lid. Boil for 1 hr. Pour out all but 250ml (or a 3cm deep puddle) of the spiced cooking liquid. Preheat your oven to 200°C/Gas 6.

Peel and thinly slice your apples (discarding seeds and stem). Lay them, with the potatoes and onions, in a roasting tin and place the gammon on top, fat-side facing up. Pour in the spiced liquid from the pan. Scatter the sage leaves over the top. Dust the sugar over the top of the gammon. Roast for 45 mins or till the fat is a little golden and crackly on top.

Cashew, Turmeric & Date Dressing

We've reached the golden age of the season. Once you whip up this magnificent dressing you'll want to smother every winter veg going in it. From smoked beetroot or roasted celeriac to hearty greens like blanched kale and fresh watercress.

Vg ⚒ 5 MINS, PLUS OVERNIGHT SOAKING (IF POSSIBLE) 🍲 0 (OR 5 MINS) 🍴 4-6

100g cashews (soaked overnight, if possible)

1 Medjool date, stoned

3cm turmeric root, peeled or 1 tsp ground turmeric

A pinch of chilli powder

150-200ml cold water

Sea salt

If you didn't have time to soak your cashews overnight, simmer them for 5 mins in enough water to cover. Drain. Rinse under cold water. Pop in a blender with the date, turmeric, chilli powder and a pinch of sea salt. Whizz till smooth, trickling in the water till it's the consistency of double cream. Taste. Add more salt or chilli, or turmeric, as needed.

Winter Salsa Verde

Kale tips its hat to parsley here in this classic Italian condiment that's extra marvellous when dolloped next to fish or tossed with fresh pasta and a nugget of butter. In the spring, swap out the kale with the leafy green tops of bunched carrots.

 V 5 MINS NIL 4-6 1

200g kale

50g anchovies or pitted olives

1 tbsp capers

1 large garlic clove

1 lemon, zest (and juice, optional)

A hint of chilli (optional)

1-3 tbsp olive oil

Strip your kale leaves from their woody stalks. Wash well. Pile into a food processor or get a sharp knife at the ready. Blitz or chop to the consistency of finely chopped parsley.

Add the anchovies (or olives), capers, garlic, lemon zest and chilli (if using) into the mix. Add enough olive oil (and a little water or lemon juice) till as thick or as thin as you like.

Gorgeous tossed with pasta, served alongside roast mutton, or simply drizzled over toasted sourdough.

Kale Pancakes with Tahini Butter

Billowy, bountiful kale meets beautiful batter in this great green takeover of American-style pancakes. Blitzing up kale leaves with the batter gives them their lush colour and the tahini flavoured butter is a superb topping.

 V 15 MINS 25 MINS 4 ½

50g salted butter, softened

25g tahini

1 tsp honey

75g kale

3 eggs

150ml milk (any kind)

150g plain flour

2 heaped tsp baking powder

30g caster sugar

Coconut oil, for frying

Sea salt

Mash the butter, tahini and honey in a bowl with a fork till well mixed. Pop in the fridge to chill while you make the pancakes.

Tear the kale leaves off the thick middle cores. Put the leaves, eggs and milk in a blender. Blitz till combined and smooth.

Sift the flour and baking powder into a bowl. Add the sugar and a pinch of salt. Pour in the kale mix and whisk to make a smooth batter.

Set your oven to its lowest temperature.

Warm 1 tsp of coconut oil in a large frying pan over a medium heat. Add 2 tbsp of batter per pancake to the pan - you should be able to cook two or three pancakes at a time. Gently fry for 3 mins till browned underneath with lots of bubbles on top.

Flip. Cook for another 1-2 mins till set. Keep warm on a plate in the oven while you cook the rest of the pancakes, adding more oil as you need it. You should get 16-20 pancakes. Serve them in stacks topped with the chilled tahini butter.

Parsnip & Apple Pancakes

Pair this quick batter with apple, cinnamon and parsnip and you'll want to stack these pancakes very high on your plate indeed.

 15 MINS 30 MINS 4 ½

1 medium parsnip

1 apple

A squeeze of lemon juice

30g caster sugar

1 tsp ground cinnamon

3 eggs

150ml milk (any kind)

150g plain flour

2 tsp baking powder

Coconut oil, for frying

A knob of butter, to serve

A drizzle of honey, to serve

Sea salt

Peel and coarsely grate the parsnip and apple. Pop in a bowl with a squeeze of lemon juice, the caster sugar and the cinnamon.

Whisk the eggs and milk together in a jug. Sift the flour and baking powder into a bowl with a pinch of salt. Slowly pour the milk mixture into the flour, whisking as you go to make a smooth, thick batter with a consistency similar to double cream. Fold in the parsnip and apple.

Set your oven to its lowest temperature.

Warm 1 tsp of coconut oil in a large frying pan over a medium heat. Add 1 tbsp of batter per pancake to the pan - you should be able to cook 3-5 pancakes at a time. Fry for 3-4 mins, then carefully turn over and fry for another 2-3 mins till golden and cooked through.

Slide the pancakes onto a plate and keep warm in the oven while you cook the rest of them, adding more oil as you need it. You should get 16-20 pancakes. Serve them in a stack topped with butter and a drizzle of honey.

Winter Woodland Dolmades

Whether you like walking in a winter wonderland or would rather embrace the great indoors, you can't beat a little Greek inspiration. Seasonal venison, cavolo nero, shiitake mushrooms, nuts and berries form the talented chorus in this production.

 20 MINS 🍲 1 HR 30 MINS 🍴 4-6 ❤ 1

75g brown basmati rice

Olive oil

1 onion, finely chopped

100g shiitake mushrooms, finely chopped

1 tbsp ground cumin

1 tsp ground cinnamon

A pinch of chilli powder

250g venison mince

A large handful of flat leaf parsley, roughly chopped

4 tbsp walnut halves, roughly chopped

2 tbsp dried cranberries

1 lemon, zest and juice, plus extra slices to serve

1 ltr chicken or vegetable stock

16 large cavolo nero leaves

Chilli sauce, to serve (optional)

Sea salt and freshly ground pepper

Tip the rice into a bowl. Add enough cold water to cover. Set aside.

Set a frying pan over a medium heat. Add a splash of oil to the pan. Swirl in the onion and a pinch of salt. Cook for 5 mins, or till translucent.

Add the mushrooms to the onions. Cook for 5–10 mins or till they pick up a little colour. Add the cumin, cinnamon, chilli powder and the venison mince. Turn the heat up to high. Sizzle till the meat is nicely browned, stirring to break up any lumps. Season to taste.

Drain the rice. Add it to the meat and take off the heat (the rice will cook when you steam the filled parcels). Add the parsley and walnuts to the meat mixture along with the cranberries and the zest of 1 lemon.

Bring your stock to the boil. Trim the base off your cavolo nero leaves so they're roughly 18cm long. Plunge the leaves into the stock (you may have to do this in batches). Remove with tongs or a slotted spoon, saving the stock for later. Let the leaves cool for a moment.

Pour enough olive oil to coat the base into a large lidded pan. Then start filling. For each dolma, add 1 heaped tbsp of filling in the centre of one leaf. Roll up securely, folding the sides over the mix as you roll. If the filling tries to escape from the sides, roll another leaf around the parcel, in the opposite direction, to cover the sides.

Arrange the stuffed parcels, seam side-down, in the pan coated with olive oil. Create a double layer of dolmades if you need to.

Set a sieve over the top. Squeeze the juice from the zested lemon over the dolmades (the sieve will catch the pips). Pour enough stock over to just cover. Bring to the boil. Lower the heat. Pop a lid on. Simmer for 1 hr.

Carefully remove the steamed parcels from the pot, allowing two or three per serving. Spoon any excess broth over, too. Delicious on their own with fresh lemon slices, or serve with a splash of chilli sauce, or garlicky crème fraîche.

Celeriac Couscous

You can pretty much turn any hearty root veg (and even a squash) into couscous. Simply peel, make sure you use a knife to peel celeriac as it'll wreck your veg peeler. Rinse and roughly chop. Pile into a food processor and blitz till it looks like couscous. No food processor? Just finely grate. To cook, spoon into a large pan with 3–4 tbsp water, 1 tbsp olive oil or butter, and a good pinch of salt and pepper. Stir over medium heat till tender and steamed through, about 5 mins. Add a little lemon zest and juice and fresh thyme leaves.

Celeriac Soup with a Zesty Kick

Winter citrus is a lifesaver when it comes to adding a bit of sunshine and zest to the season. Here, it livens up one of our great British eccentrics, celeriac. While it may not win a beauty contest, we love it for it's rooty goodness.

 15 MINS 30 MINS 4 2

1 celeriac

1 tbsp olive oil

1 onion, finely chopped

A handful of coriander, leaves and stalks separated

1 garlic clove, grated

3cm ginger, grated

1 chilli, deseeded and finely chopped

1 lime, zest and juice

900ml veg stock

Sea salt and freshly ground pepper

Carve the peel off the celeriac. Roughly chop it.

Warm a large pan for 1 min over a medium heat. Add the oil and the chopped celeriac and onion. Season. Cover. Sweat over a low heat for 10 mins.

Finely chop the coriander stalks.

Stir the garlic, ginger, chilli, coriander stalks and lime zest into the veg. Add the stock. Cover, turn the heat up and bring to the boil.

Turn the heat down a little and simmer for 15 mins till the veg are soft.

Ladle the veg into a blender and blitz till smooth (or use a handheld blender in the pan).

Swirl in the lime juice. Taste and add more salt and pepper if it needs it. Serve in warm bowls, and top with the coriander leaves.

Celeriac Noodles with Mushroom Pesto

Rachel is a magician. She's turned celeriac into noodles, and it's incredible. There's a choir of people singing this recipe's praises here. It's easy and all you need is a knife and a veg peeler.

 20 MINS 15 MINS 4 2

100g walnuts, plus a few extra to garnish

250g mushrooms

A large handful of parsley, plus extra to garnish

1 tsp fresh thyme leaves

1 garlic clove

1 lemon, zest and juice

4–6 tbsp olive oil, plus a gloss to serve

1 small or ½ large celeriac

Sea salt and freshly ground pepper

Preheat your oven to 200°C/Gas 6. Put a large roasting tray on the top shelf to heat up.

Put everything up to the lemon zest into a blender or food processor. Add a squeeze of lemon juice. Drizzle in 4 tbsp of olive oil and season. Pulse till you have a coarse pesto, not too smooth. Add more oil or lemon juice to bring it together, if needed. Set aside.

Halve your celeriac. Carve the peel off. Cut into 1–2cm panels. The thinner your panels, the thinner your noodles will be.

Use a veg peeler to shave long ribbons (these are your noodles) from the side of each panel you've cut. You may be left with a few stumpy ends that you can't noodle, which is fine. Use them in stock.

Pile your ribbons into a bowl. Rinse them. Add a squeeze of lemon juice.

Massage half the pesto into the noodles. Add more pesto till the noodles are generously coated. Arrange them in a single layer on your hot roasting tray.

Roast on the top shelf for 15 mins or till tender (it's nice if a few noodles go a little crisp around the edges). Give them a mix halfway through to help them cook evenly.

Pile them onto plates. Finish with a gloss of olive oil, a little salt, pepper, more parsley and a few walnut pieces scattered over the top.

Mutton Mince Pie

This rich mutton pie is based on an eighteenth-century English recipe for mince pies, and teams organic mutton with festive dried fruits and spices. If you like Moroccan tagines, then you will love this sweet and savoury twist on the mince pie.

🥄 40 MINS, PLUS AT LEAST 30 MINS' CHILLING (UP TO OVERNIGHT) 🍲 1 HR 15 MINS, PLUS 15 MINS' COOLING 🍴 6-8

For the pastry:

250g plain flour, plus extra for dusting

150g cold butter

2-3 tbsp cold water

Sea salt

For the filling:

A knob of butter, for greasing

1 tbsp olive oil

400g mutton mince

150g apples

2cm ginger, grated

50g walnut halves, finely chopped

1 tsp cinnamon

¼ tsp ground cloves

½ whole nutmeg

75g raisins

2 heaped tbsp sugar

2 tbsp cognac

1 egg, beaten (or 2 tbsp milk), for glazing

Sift the flour into a bowl. Chop in the cold butter and use your fingertips to rub it in to make fine breadcrumbs. Add a pinch of salt and enough cold water that you can stir it together into a soft dough. Wrap and chill in the fridge for at least 30 mins, or overnight.

Preheat your oven to 220°C/Gas 7 and place a baking tray in there to heat up. Butter a deep, loose-bottomed 20cm cake tin. Heat the olive oil in a large frying pan. Add the mutton. Fry for 10-12 mins, stirring occasionally, till the mince is browned. Pour off any excess liquid.

While the mince fries, peel, core and grate the apples. Add the apples, ginger, walnuts, cinnamon and ground cloves to a bowl. Grate in the nutmeg. Add the raisins, sugar and cognac. Mix well. Taste and add a pinch of salt if you think it needs it. Set aside to cool.

Slice off one-third of the pastry and set aside. Dust your work surface with flour and roll out the larger chunk to make a circle approximately 25cm across. Use it to line the cake tin, making sure it comes all the way up the sides and folding down any excess over the edge. Spoon the mutton filling into the pastry case. Roll out the remaining pastry to make a 20cm round. Lay it on top of the pie filling and use a fork to crimp the pastry edges together.

Brush the top of the pie with beaten egg or milk and place the tin on the hot baking tray in the oven. Bake for 50 mins to 1 hr till golden. Cool in the tin for 15 mins, then run a knife around the edges to loosen the pie. Lift out of the tin. Serve warm, in slices, with buttered cabbage and gravy, or cold as part of a Boxing Day buffet.

Blood Orange Piri Piri Chicken

Piri piri chicken is a Portuguese classic. Sorrel's version, with new season blood oranges, is the new-improved classic that'll bring a ray of cheer to even the most melancholic Fado.

 25 MINS   55 MINS   4-6   2

1 tbsp olive oil
4 chicken thighs
1 blood orange

For the piri piri sauce:
1 onion
1 red pepper
1 red chilli
1 tsp olive oil
2 garlic cloves
2 tsp dried oregano
1 tbsp red wine vinegar
1 blood orange
100ml cold water
Sea salt and freshly ground pepper

Start by making the piri piri sauce. Heat your grill to its highest setting. Peel the onion and cut into eight wedges. Cut the pepper in half and scoop out the seeds. Pull the stalk from the chilli.

Line a large baking tray with foil and arrange the onion, pepper and chilli on it. Drizzle the onion wedges with 1 tbsp of oil. Add the garlic cloves (whole and unpeeled).

Grill for 10 mins. Turn the chilli over and grill for another 5-10 mins till everything is charred.

Preheat your oven to 220°C/Gas 7.

Pop the pepper halves and chilli in a bowl and cover with cling film. Leave for 5 mins to cool, then carefully peel off the blackened skin (don't worry if some skin stays attached). For a less spicy dish, slice open the chilli and scrape out the seeds and white bits. Carefully squeeze the grilled garlic from its skin.

Put the pepper, chilli, garlic and onion into a food processor. Add the oregano and vinegar. Squeeze in the juice from the blood orange. Add the water. Season and blitz. No processor? Finely chop the veg and stir with the oregano, vinegar, orange juice and water.

Drizzle 1 tbsp of oil over the chicken. Rub the oil into the skin of each thigh and season. Heat a griddle or frying pan till it's hot. Add the chicken thighs, skin-side down. Fry for 3–4 mins till the skin is crisp.

Transfer to a roasting tin, skin-side up. Spoon over the piri piri sauce. Cut the blood orange into eight wedges and nestle around the chicken. Roast for 40 mins till the chicken is cooked through.

Dining Circles

Organic chooks have the tastiest diet, which in turn makes them even more delicious. Most non-organic chickens are fed genetically modified (GM) ingredients. Organic certification means this isn't the case. They also get plenty of sunshine, which gives them (and you) more vitamin D.

Preserved Bergamot Lemons

Winter's bundle of citrus includes fragrant bergamot lemons (yes, the ones they use to flavour Earl Grey). A gorgeous and quick way to bundle them away for future use is to preserve them in salt, like the Moroccans do. Gorgeous in tagines, of course, but also stunning whipped into an instant soup with a peeled ripe pear, a large handful of baby leaf spinach and enough stock to bring it all together.

 10 MINS 0 MAKES: 1KG

6 bergamot lemons
6–8 tbsp sea salt
1 cinnamon stick
2 bay leaves

Quarter your lemons. Tumble into a large bowl. Dust 1 tbsp of salt over the top. Rub the salt into the lemons, extracting and squeezing the juice out as you do so.

Strain the lemons from the juice (but keep the juice!).

Layer the lemons, cinnamon and bay in sterilised jars (see page 114) – you will need three 350ml jars or a large 1-litre jar. Sprinkle over enough salt to cover each layer (about 1 tbsp) – you'll have about six layers.

Pour the strained lemon juice over the top of the final layer of salt. It should cover everything. If not, top up with boiling water. Seal the jars. Leave in a dark, cool place for a month, shaking it every week or so.

The lemons are now ready to use. Store in the fridge once opened, keeping the lemons covered with the brine. Use within 6 months of opening.

No Chemical Sprays Here

When preserving or zesting citrus, always go organic to ensure you get pure, nutritious peels.

Did you know, the more sunshine a hen has seen, the paler the egg?

Eggs naturally have different hues. Paler eggs can be graded out by big farms, but we see no need.

Our superb organic eggs come to us from Wiltshire. The lucky cluckers have a truly free-range life, and because of this, our eggs vary in colour as the clouds drift on by and we adore these little quirks of nature.

Honeyed Orange & Polenta Pancakes

A delicious, gluten- and dairy-free take on classic, American-style pancakes. Always use organic polenta. Polenta is often made from GM crops.

(V) 🥄 10 MINS, PLUS 10 MINS' RESTING   🍲 10 MINS   🍴 4   ❤ 1 (IF SERVED WITH ORANGE SEGMENTS)

4 egg whites (see tip)

100g polenta

150ml orange juice (plus zest if using fresh juice)

2 tsp baking powder

2 tsp ground cinnamon

2 tbsp honey, plus extra for serving

A gloss of oil, for frying

A knob of butter or coconut oil, to serve

3–4 blood or navel oranges, in segments, to serve

Sea salt

Place your egg whites in a glass or metal bowl. Add a pinch of salt. Whisk with a strong arm or use a hand mixer till the eggs are meringue-like stiff, glossy and fluffy.

Gently fold the polenta, orange juice and zest (if using fresh juice), baking powder, cinnamon and 2 tbsp of honey into the eggs. Let the batter set for 10 mins to thicken up.

Get a large frying pan hot over a medium heat, gloss with oil and dollop 1–2 tbsp of the mix into the pan per pancake. You should be able to cook two or three pancakes at a time. Fry till golden on the underneath, only 1–2 mins. Turn over and fry for another 1–2 mins on the other side.

Serve with butter (or a dairy-free alternative like coconut oil) and a generous drizzle of honey. Beautiful with wintry segments of orange on the side.

Good Yolks

Put your leftover yolks to good use by whipping up hollandaise or homemade mayo, or freeze in ice cube trays (for up to 6 months) and use the defrosted yolks to brush over pastry.

Bombay Beetroot Salad

As bright as a Bollywood dance sequence, you'll love this spiced salad. For extra warmth, fold the grated veg through the warm oil while it's still in the pan, just to heat things up a little.

 15 MINS 5 MINS 4 ½

3cm ginger

2 tbsp olive oil

1 lime, zest and juice

2 garlic cloves, thinly sliced

1 tsp black mustard seeds

1 tsp ground turmeric

2 carrots, peeled and coarsely grated

400g beetroot, peeled and coarsely grated

A large handful of coriander, leaves and stalks separated

Sea salt and freshly ground pepper

Peel and cut the ginger into thin slices. Cut the slices into matchsticks.

Heat a small pan. When warm, pour in the olive oil. Add the lime zest, ginger, garlic and mustard seeds. Sprinkle in the turmeric and a pinch of salt and pepper. Swirl everything together. Cook for 2 mins till the garlic and ginger are crispy.

Whisk in the lime juice. Fold in the grated veg.

Finely chop the coriander stalks. Stir into the veg. Pile into bowls. Scatter the coriander leaves over the top, to serve.

Baked Golden Beetroot Risotto with Roasted Garlic Cream

We've gone for the golden boy of the beetroot family for this dish. Burpees Golden is the variety. It was all the rage in Victorian times and we're keen to bring it back into fashion. Try it, especially in this sunny risotto. We guarantee, it will tickle you pink without staining your hands.

 V · 10 MINS · 45-50 MINS · 4 · 1

1 garlic bulb

2 tbsp olive oil

1 onion, finely chopped

400g golden beetroot, scrubbed and coarsely grated

200g risotto rice

750ml veg or chicken stock, warmed

A handful of thyme, leaves only

200g crème fraîche

1 tbsp Dijon mustard

A handful of flat leaf parsley, stalks and leaves, finely chopped

Sea salt and freshly ground pepper

Preheat your oven to 200°C/Gas 6.

Pull one clove of garlic from the bulb and set aside. Wrap the bulb in foil and pop it in the oven to roast for about 40 mins.

Set a large pan over a medium heat. Add 1 tbsp of the oil. Add the onion. Season with salt and pepper. Fry for 5 mins till the onion is soft and glossy. Stir often.

Peel and crush the reserved garlic clove. Stir the beetroot, crushed garlic and risotto rice into the onion. Stir in the warmed stock and thyme leaves. Bring to the boil, then ladle the risotto into a casserole or ovenproof dish.

Pop a lid on the casserole dish or cover it tightly with foil. Bake for 30 mins till the rice is soft. Remove the lid or foil and cook for another 5-10 mins till the risotto has dried out a little.

The roasted garlic bulb should be softened. Squeeze half the flesh from the skins using the back of a knife. Stir it through the crème fraîche with the Dijon mustard and plenty of salt and pepper. Add more garlic to taste.

Taste the risotto and adjust the seasoning. Swirl half the roasted garlic and mustard cream through it, with some of the chopped parsley. Top with the remaining garlicky cream and a garnish of parsley. Delicious with a simple salad.

Getting Clove-r

Wrap the remaining roasted garlic in foil and keep in the fridge for up to 3 days. Spread a roasted garlic clove or two on hot toast, or stir into soups, stews or risottos. Incidentally, chewing parsley helps to freshen the breath.

Oak-Smoked Leeks

When just about all the leaves have drifted from your local oak trees, gather a few branches and pile them into a pot to make this dish – the most stunning leeks you'll ever rest your fork on. Delicious as a side for a wintry Sunday roast (stunning with beef and a side of creamed horseradish), or whipped into a leek and potato soup for an oaky, smoky twist.

 5 MINS 15-20 MINS 4 1

3-4 leeks

150g rice (any kind)

5-6 smallish oak branches

2 tbsp water

Drizzle of olive oil, to serve

1 lemon, juice, to serve

Sea salt and freshly ground pepper, to serve

Get a large lidded pot (cast iron casserole dishes are ideal, but not essential). Line with two layers of foil to protect the base of the pan.

Wash and trim your leeks. If they're really long, cut into lengths long enough to fit in your pot.

Scatter the rice in the base of the pot. You want enough to just coat the bottom (about 1cm deep). Arrange the oak branches on top. Nestle the leeks on the oak branches. Sprinkle with the water. Set over a high heat. Pop the lid on your pot.

Once the pan starts smoking, set a timer for 10 mins. Let the leeks smoke for that long. Take off the heat but leave the lid on and let them lap up more smoke for a further 5-10 mins before serving.

Thinly slice, puree or serve whole. Lovely with a little salt, pepper, olive oil and lemon juice, or whip into your favourite leek dish.

Cleaning up the Leeks

Here's the easiest way to get that organic soil off your leeks. With a sharp knife, slice the leek from just above the white bit to the tops of the leaves. Then hold under running water whilst separating the leaves a little.

Ginger Sesame Leek Rice

This side goes exceptionally well with leftover shredded meat, pan-fried fish or tofu. Or give it a top hat of a poached egg and drizzle with some chilli oil.

 V∅ 10 MINS 25-30 MINS 4 1

300g brown rice

Olive oil

700ml water or stock

4-6 tbsp sesame seeds

3-4 leeks

3cm ginger

Sea salt and freshly ground pepper

Get a lidded pot hot. Add your rice. Toast for a moment. Swirl in a gloss of oil and a pinch of salt. Add your water or stock. Pop the lid on and lower the heat.

Cook for 20 mins or till all the water is absorbed. Trickle in a bit more water if it absorbs too quickly. Keep the lid on and steam for a further 5-10 mins.

Get a large frying pan hot. Toast your sesame seeds for a mo. Tumble onto a plate. Set aside.

Trim the rooty end off your leeks. Thinly slice till you get up to the tougher dark green bits - use this bit for stock.

Rinse your sliced leeks. Cook in a splash or two of oil, with a good hit of salt and pepper, till the leeks are really tender.

Chop a slice off your piece of ginger, and julienne (matchstick) it. Freshly grate the rest. Fold 1 tbsp of grated ginger through your cooked rice. Taste. Add more ginger if you wish. Swirl in half the leeks and half the sesame seeds.

Pile into bowls. Finish with the remaining leeks and sesame seeds and a few wisps of julienned ginger. Add a gloss of oil before serving. Beautiful!

Feta Than Ever

This is also stunning served with a dollop of whipped feta (blend 100g of natural yogurt with 100g of feta till smooth and creamy, whip in a little water if needed), watercress and toasted walnuts.

Majestic Spiced Kale & Pomegranate

Deliciously tender blanched kale, a gloss of garlicky olive oil, a hint of exotic spice and the punch of pomegranate make for a colourful festive side dish.

 15 MINS 7 MINS 6-8 1

400g kale

2 tbsp olive oil

2 garlic cloves, thinly sliced

1 tsp ras el hanout or ground cumin

1 pomegranate

Sea salt and freshly ground pepper

Bring a large pot of water to the boil. Tug the kale leaves from their woody stalks. Roughly chop or tear any big kale leaves.

Plunge the kale into the boiling water. Swirl through. Cook for just 1 min or till bright, glossy green. Drain. Set aside.

Put your pan back on the heat. Add the oil to the pan. Swirl the sliced garlic through the oil, with a pinch of salt. Cook the garlic till just golden. Add the kale and spice. Swirl through to mix. Taste. Add a little salt and pepper, to taste.

Halve your pomegranate. Remove the seeds (see tip). Arrange the kale on a platter. Scatter the pomegranate seeds over the top.

Shake Your Pom Poms

Turn the pomegranate inside out and gently tease the seeds out with your fingers. Catch the escaping juices in a bowl.

Jewelled Chocolate Torte

A showstopper of a cake, this rich dark chocolate cake has a moreishly
squidgy middle. A big scattering of pomegranate seeds adds a splash of
colour and juiciness.

 V · 20 MINS, PLUS FREEZING OVERNIGHT · 25-30 MINS · 6

Sunflower or olive oil, for greasing

200g dark chocolate (70%)

150g unsalted butter, at room temperature

150g caster sugar

4 eggs

2 tbsp plain flour

1 level tsp ground cinnamon

35g ground almonds

1 pomegranate

Crème fraîche, to serve

Heat your oven to 180°C/Gas 4. Brush the bottom and sides of a
20cm loose-bottomed cake tin with oil. Line the base of the tin
with baking paper.

Break up the chocolate. Put it in a heatproof bowl. Half-fill a pan
with boiling water. Pop the bowl in the pan so it sits on top but the
water doesn't touch the bottom of the bowl. Gently heat for 2-3
mins till the chocolate melts.

In a bowl, beat the butter and sugar together with an electric beater
or a wooden spoon for 2-3 mins, till pale and fluffy. Beat the eggs in
a separate bowl. A little at a time, add the eggs into the butter and
beat well. If the mix looks like it'll curdle, add a spoonful of the flour.

Sieve the flour into the mix with the ground cinnamon. Add the
melted chocolate and ground almonds. Use a flexible spatula to lift
and fold the cake mixture together.

Scrape the cake mixture into the tin. Bake for 25-30 mins till it's just
set with a little wobble in the middle and has formed a crust. Leave
the cake to cool in the tin. Pop it in the freezer overnight (this helps
make the texture fudgy). Or, freeze for up to 1 month if you really
want to get ahead.

Defrost the cake for a few hours before serving. Slather the crème
fraîche over the top of the cake. Quarter the pomegranate. Scoop
out the seeds. Scatter them over the cake and serve.

Butterscotch & Parsnip Pud

Puds are for life, not just for Christmas. This veggie twist on a traditional pudding will go with just about any winter roast. Just remember to play nice so everyone can have a bit. Keep it gluten-free by using buckwheat flour.

 V 20 MINS 1HR 6-8 ½

For the pud:

100g unsalted butter, plus extra for greasing

100g buckwheat flour, plus extra for dusting

200ml strongly brewed black tea or Earl Grey

1 tbsp vanilla extract or seeds from ½ vanilla pod

1 tbsp freshly grated ginger

2 tsp ground cinnamon

1 tsp ground cloves

1 tsp mixed spice

200g Medjool dates, pitted

½ tsp bicarbonate of soda

1 tsp baking powder

125g ground almonds

150g parsnips, peeled and coarsely grated

75g crystallised ginger, roughly chopped

100g walnuts, toasted and roughly chopped

125g Demerara sugar

2 tbsp black treacle

1 large egg

For the butterscotch:

150ml double cream

100g unsalted butter, at room temperature

1 tsp black treacle or honey

Sea salt

Preheat your oven to 180°C/Gas 4. Lightly butter your pudding basin. Dust with just enough flour to lightly coat. Tip out any excess flour.

In a pan, mix the tea, vanilla, ginger, cinnamon, cloves, mixed spice, dates and bicarbonate of soda. Gently simmer over a low heat till the dates are softened. Mush the dates with a spoon or fork to further break them up into a rustic date puree.

Toss the buckwheat flour, baking powder, ground almonds, grated parsnip, crystallised ginger and walnuts together in a large bowl.

In a separate bowl, whisk the sugar and the treacle for the pudding and the butter together till light and fluffy. Whip the egg into the mix.

Spoon the butter and date mixtures into the flour. Gently fold everything together till evenly mixed.

Spoon the pudding into the pudding basin. Smooth with the back of a spoon. Cover the top with a layer of foil and pop in the centre of the oven. Bake for 1 hr or till a knife inserted in the centre comes out clean.

For the butterscotch, in a bowl whip the cream and butter together, with the treacle or honey, till thick and creamy. Spoon into a pan. Add a pinch of salt. Gently warm over a low heat, whisking the whole time, till all the sugar has dissolved. Leave to cool a little, to allow it to thicken. If the butterscotch splits, give it a good whisk to bring it back together.

Spoon the butterscotch over the warm pud.

Here's One we Made Earlier...

The pud can be made weeks in advance and frozen, or up to 3 days ahead if stored in the fridge. Just pop it back in the oven to warm through before serving.

Coconut Sugar Caramel Blood Oranges

Just when you thought winter citrus couldn't be improved upon (they're practically a pud all by themselves after all), out steps some cardamom-studded salted caramel to accompany them, and all bets are off.

10 MINS   5 MINS   4   1½

6 blood oranges (or any orange, mandarin or clementine)

125g coconut sugar

Ground seeds from 2 cardamom pods

2 tbsp boiling water

Sea salt

If you're using oranges, cut a slice off the top and bottom of each one, then slice the peel off the sides. If you're using clementines, simply peel them. Thinly slice the citrus fruit and arrange on a platter or plates.

Pour the coconut sugar into a heavy-based pan (cast iron is ideal). Add the ground cardamom seeds. Set over a medium heat. Keep an eagle eye on it.

Stir in the water once the sugar has half-melted – be careful as it may sputter up. Add a pinch of sea salt. Let it cook for 30 seconds. Drizzle over your orange slices. Serve warm or at room temperature.

A Zest for Life

We literally jump for joy each year when the citrus season begins. Much of our crop comes from a chap called Giangiacomo. His Sicilian organic groves overlook Mt Etna. Ever seen a greenish looking orange this time of year? Citrus fruits need warm days and chilly evenings to get their signature colour, but they still taste fantastic whatever their hue.

Red Velvet Truffles

These truffles are crackers, dairy-free and even have a bit of veg in them. The beetroot turns them a beautiful velvety shade of red.

 15 MINS 5 MINS MAKES: ABOUT 12

200ml beetroot juice (see tip)

2 tbsp coconut oil

Seeds from ½ vanilla pod, or ½ tsp vanilla extract

½ tsp ground cinnamon

Ground seeds from 3 cardamom pods

A pinch of chilli powder

250g dark chocolate

100g cocoa powder, to coat

Sea salt

Warm the beetroot juice, coconut oil, vanilla, cinnamon, cardamom, chilli and a pinch of salt in a large saucepan till steamy. Break your chocolate into small pieces. Take the beetroot juice off the heat. Cool for 2 mins, then stir in the chocolate till it's fully melted and incorporated.

If the mixture splits, vigorously whisk in 1-2 tsp of cold water till it's silky smooth and creamy again. Pop the mixture in the fridge till set.

Scoop up rounded teaspoons of truffle mixture. Roll into balls.

Tip the cocoa powder into a dish. Roll the truffles through the cocoa powder to coat. Chill till ready to serve.

Get the Beet

You can use fresh or bottled beetroot juice. For fresh beetroot juice, you'll need about 300–350g of raw beetroot to yield 200ml of juice.

Spiced Gingerbread Truffles

Gingerbread is simply one of those things that instantly conjures up childhood memories of Christmas. These 'grown-up' gingerbread truffles make for a fantastic homemade gift. Or, keep them for yourself and dish up with the after-dinner mints.

  20 MINS, PLUS 40 MINS' FREEZING + CHILLING 5 MINS MAKES: 15-20 1

20 Medjool dates, pitted and roughly chopped

1 tsp ground ginger

½ tsp cinnamon

Seeds from 1 vanilla pod

50g ground almonds

1 orange, zest and 2 tbsp juice

3cm ginger, grated

100g dark chocolate (at least 70%)

½ tsp coconut oil

Put the dates in a food processor with all the other ingredients except the chocolate and coconut oil. Pulse till you have a smooth mix. It will look a bit like caramel. Scoop it out into a bowl and pop in the freezer to firm up for 30 mins.

Scoop up the mix by the teaspoon, giving you a rough rugby ball shape. It doesn't matter if the balls are a little rustic. Lay them on a flat tray and pop in the freezer again for 10 mins.

Break the chocolate into small pieces and melt with the coconut oil in a small bowl over a pan of simmering water. Leave to cool slightly.

Drop a ball into the melted chocolate and roll it around with a spoon to cover it entirely. Lift out with the spoon, allowing any excess chocolate to drip off. Place on a lined baking tray. Repeat with the remaining mixture. Pop in the fridge to allow the chocolate to set.

Juiced Rubies

Ditch the off-the-shelf bottled stuff and make your own homemade juice using fresh, seasonal pomegranates with a hint of lime.

 5-10 MINS 0 2 1

2 pomegranates
1 lime, zest and juice
400ml cold water

Cut the pomegranates in half.

Hold the pomegranate in the palm of your hand over a bowl. Whack the back of the pomegranate with a wooden spoon and the seeds should fall through your fingers along with any juice.

Repeat with the other halves.

Add the lime zest and juice to the bowl. Add the cold water. Pour into a high-speed blender and whizz till smooth. Pour through a sieve to remove any gritty seeds if you like.

Spiced Ale Flip

Warm the cockles with this delicious mulled ale flip. Once upon a December this was made with rum, sugar and a red-hot poker. The poker's busy with the fire, so we've kept the booze and sweet stuff, but used the hob instead.

 5 MINS 5-10 MINS 2

1 lemon, juice
1cm fresh ginger, finely grated
30g caster sugar
½ tsp cinnamon
500ml beer
50ml rum
1 large egg
Whole nutmeg, for grating (optional)

Pour the lemon juice into a pan. Add the ginger, sugar, cinnamon and beer. Place over a low heat (don't boil it) and stir till the beer is steaming hot and the sugar has dissolved. Pour through a sieve to strain out the ginger.

In a separate, large pan, whisk the rum and egg together till well combined.

Take the beer off the heat. Slowly whisk a few small ladlefuls of the beer into the egg (don't add it too quickly or you will scramble the egg). Whisk in all the beer. Once everything is combined, pour the mixture back into the original pan, then pour it back again. Do this three or four times, pouring backwards and forwards, till the ale is foamy and the colour of tea. Alternatively, keep it in one pan and give it a good whisk till it's foamy.

Pour the ale flip into two cups or heatproof beer glasses. If you like nutmeg, grate a little over the top before serving.

RIDICULOUSLY QUICK RECIPES

Persian Pomegranate Pots

Melt 50g of white chocolate in a bowl set over a saucepan of simmering water. Fold the melted chocolate through 200g of crème fraîche. Add a hint of vanilla (seeds or extract) and cardamom. Top with a sprinkle of pomegranate seeds, a drop of rosewater and a handful of pistachios.

Parsnip, Hazelnut & Sage Hash

Scrub or peel about 2 or 3 parsnips. Coarsely grate. Fry in a little oil with crushed hazelnuts and 3 or 4 finely chopped sage leaves. Delicious with pan-fried sea bass and orange butter (boil the juice of 1 orange down to 1 tbsp and whisk in 1 tbsp of butter).

Mushroom Pot Noodle

Thinly slice a few handfuls or a punnet of mushrooms (any type). Arrange on a clean tea towel. Set in a warm, dry place for 2-3 days or till fully dried. Then toss into a pot with rice noodles, chilli flakes and a dollop of miso. Top up with hot water. Steep for 10 mins. Finish with a sprinkling of chives.

Cumin, Beet & Orange Carpaccio

Peel and thinly slice 1 or 2 beetroot (the smaller, the better). Toss with salt, pepper, the juice and zest of 1 orange and 1 tbsp of olive oil. Peel and thinly slice 1 or 2 oranges. Arrange on a platter with the beetroot. Finish with a sprinkling of toasted cumin seeds and pumpkin seeds.

Coconut-Creamed Kale

Wash your kale. Strip the leaves from the woody stalks (thinly slice the woody stems and use to make a quick pickle – see page 264). Finely chop the kale. Warm 400g of coconut milk with 1 tbsp of grated ginger, a finely chopped garlic clove and a pinch of finely chopped chilli. Add the kale. Simmer till tender. Delicious with noodles, fish or dished up alongside chicken, rubbed and roasted with curry spices.

Coconut & Chilli Sprouts

Toss your quartered or halved Brussels sprouts into a hot wok with 1 or 2 tbsp of coconut oil (this is a surprisingly superb match for sprouts). Season with salt, pepper and a pinch of chilli flakes. Sizzle till a little golden around the edges. Finish with a squeeze of lime juice. Lovely with noodles, soy sauce and leftover turkey.

SCHOOL OF VEG

Welcome to the School of Veg,
a place to learn techniques you can apply
to just about any veg life throws at you.
Once you've mastered a few skills,
you'll be writing your own cookbook.

Top Techniques

Mash, slaw, smoke, broth, kraut,
rice, whip, griddle, pickle, dry

Mash

Mash is the ultimate comfort food and a great way to pack in heaps of veg. Plus, leftover mash has endless uses.

Tubers, roots, squash and brassicas are the heroes: sweet potatoes, carrots, spuds, parsnips, swede, celeriac, beetroot, turnips and cauliflower are brilliant mashers. Orchard fruits can also be lovely added to the mix: pear and celeriac is a dream combo.

Steam, boil or roast your veg/fruit till it's mashably tender. Roasting (either whole, or peeled and cut into chunks) in a 200°C/Gas 6 oven gives an intensified flavour. Steaming is healthier and boiling is faster, especially if you chop the veg into 2–3cm chunks (peel first).

How To

Mash the cooked veg with a liquid – stock, milk (any kind), or even freshly squeezed orange juice. Tougher root veg like beetroot, swede, celeriac and carrots are best whipped into mash in a food processor or blender.

Stir in herbs, spices (or flavours like curry paste), soy sauce or mustard. Finish with butter, olive or coconut oil, if you like.

Finish your mash with crunchy or crispy things: fried onions, toasted nuts and seeds, sizzled sausagemeat pieces or spiced minced lamb.

Use it to top a pie; coat in breadcrumbs and fry up fritters – stuffed with cheese for extra oomph; or mix with flour or polenta to make a dough for griddled Irish potato-like breads.

Combos

Cauliflower mashed with a good handful of grated Parmesan cheese, topped with sage leaves that have been fried in butter till crisp.

Celeriac mashed with a peeled and diced ripe pear, a grating of lemon zest, a pinch of ground cinnamon and finely chopped leaves from 1 rosemary sprig.

Swede mash made with smoked paprika, garlic and a hint of lemon zest and juice. Finish with parsley and Marcona almonds.

Classic potato mash mixed with a roasted Bramley apple, 1 thinly sliced leek fried in oil or butter, a pinch of fresh thyme leaves, a knob of butter and a splash of cider.

Try This

Jive Time Carrot Mash & Coriander Pesto, page 14

Slaw

Slaws are one of the most delicious ways to pack loads of veg, fruit and flavour into one dish. Showcase a single fruit or veg or go wild.

Firm root veg, brassicas and even fresh fruits are all perfect for slaw. Some veg and fruits we love to slaw are: courgettes, carrots, radishes, celery, fennel, firm nectarines and peaches, apples and pears in the autumn, beetroot, celeriac, kohlrabi, cabbage, rainbow chard and kale.

How To

ROOTS: Coarsely grate.

CABBAGES: Quarter. Remove the core. Thinly slice. The bigger your knife, the easier it is to get really thin shreds. A bread knife is the best tool for the job.

LEAVES: Pile your leaves in a big stack. Roll it up. Thinly slice. Et voilà!

BULBS AND STALKS: For the likes of celery, thinly slice with a big knife. For fennel, halve or quarter your bulb, then coarsely grate or use a veg peeler to peel thin wisps.

DRESS IT UP: Go wild with vinaigrettes, citrus dressings and yogurty creations with fresh herbs or spices.

FINAL FLOURISHES: Sprinkle on toasted nuts or seeds, herbs, thin wisps of garlic, ginger or chilli fried in a little oil till crisp.

SERVE: Pack into a pitta with falafel or roasted feta. Pair with a Sunday roast as a lighter side. Cap with grilled fish, spiced skewers of lamb or halloumi. Partner with a fried egg and toasted sesame seeds. Or simply enjoy on its own.

Combos

Carrots and nectarines with fresh ginger and tahini.

Fennel with olive oil, lemon, mint and feta.

Radishes with a dressing of blended roast garlic, thyme and Greek yogurt.

Courgette with toasted coconut, lemongrass, coriander, chilli, lime and agave syrup.

Cabbage with natural yogurt, curry powder, lime and toasted cashews.

Try These

Broccoli Slaw with Red Thai Yogurt & Toasted Cashews, page 140

Bombay Beetroot Salad, page 232

Smoke

You don't need any fancy kit to get smokin' veg. It only involves a handful of things: foil, a heavy-based pot (with a lid, ideally), rice, water and veg.

Root veg and tubers are the stars here: beetroot, parsnips, carrots, celeriac, swede, Jerusalem artichokes and potatoes – the joy is that smoking them helps them to cook faster. Mushrooms are also fab smoked, as are onions, shallots and leeks.

How To

Place a double layer of foil in a heavy-based, lidded pan with plenty overhanging the edges. Tip ½ mug of rice (any kind, uncooked) on top of the foil, along with a large handful of herbs, a few strips of citrus peel and/or 1–2 tbsp of spices and/or black tea.

Add 2 tbsp of water, then place a single layer of veg on top. Bring all the edges of the foil together and seal tightly, leaving no gaps. Place a lid on top. Set on the hob over a high heat. After 3 mins you should see smoke escaping. Leave to smoke for a further 10 mins. Take off the heat and let the veg continue to cook in the residual heat for 10 mins (or longer if you can). Carefully open the package. Discard the rice and aromatics.

Strip the skin or outer layer off the veg and brush or rinse off any rice that's sticking to it. Then thinly slice, mash, puree or dice, and add to your favourite dishes. If the veg isn't cooked through as much as you'd like, finish it off in a frying pan or in the oven.

Combos

Beetroot smoked over rice mixed with the zest of 1 orange, 2 or 3 bay leaves and 1 tbsp of cloves. Thinly slice and toss into a puy lentil salad with toasted seeds.

Parsnips smoked over the leaves from 2 black tea bags and a seedless vanilla pod. Mash with a little milk and butter.

Celeriac smoked over rice with rosemary and the zest of 1 lemon. Julienne it (cut into matchsticks) for a smoky twist on remoulade.

Try This

Oak-Smoked Leeks, page 236

Broth

Broth is the same as a stock. It's just adopted a more trendy name.

Bone broths are extremely good for you. They reduce inflammation in the gut (something far too many people suffer from) and they give you a huge nutrient boost.

Just boil up some bones and/or veggies until they taste wonderful.

How To

If you're making a bone broth, the longer you cook them the better: 1–2 days in a slow cooker is ideal. But a rapid boil for 1–2 hrs is good, too.

You can make as large or as small a broth as you like. You want enough water to cover the veg/bones by 2–3cm. As a base, a mix of onions and/or garlic are key, along with carrots and celery and/or fennel. In terms of bones, you can use raw bones or cooked bones from a roasted meat or fish.

You can also add veg to bone broth, such as carrots, celery and onion, along with garlic and herbs. Keep the veg in chunky pieces as it'll overcook if it's cut too finely.

For a veg broth, chop the veg finely and cook for a short period (30 mins max). Spices like cardamom, cinnamon, allspice, fresh ginger and turmeric are great additions. You can also add mushrooms, lentils and/or barley for a richer, more intense broth.

Don't forget about fish broth, too. Bones of white fish are ideal. Simply simmer them for one hour. Lovely with fennel, onion, celery and bay leaves added to the pot.

How to Serve It

You can sip a strained broth like a tea, on its own, but we prefer treating it like a stock and adding bits and bobs like grated root veg, seasonal greens, herbs and leftover shreds of meat.

Try This

Perfect Poached Chicken & Wild Garlic Gremolata Broth, page 26

Kraut

Sauerkraut is the most famous, but you can turn all sorts of roots and brassicas into krauts. All you need to know are a few simple basics. And make sure everything you use is really clean. From there, it's a doddle.

How To

Start by finely shredding a cabbage (red, green, white, or even cauliflower leaves). Add a handful of grated roots and/or apple or pear.

Dust 1 heaped tbsp of sea salt over the top. Massage into the veg for 5 mins, then rest for 5 mins. Massage again for 5 mins. The veg should have wilted and be submerged in the brine.

Add spices to the mix, if you like. Caraway, coriander seeds, juniper, star anise, cinnamon, ginger or horseradish are just a few ideas...

Cover the surface of the kraut mix with a sheet of cling film, smoothing out any bubbles. Lay some weights on top to press the cabbage down. Then, cover the whole thing with a lid or a taut layer of cling film to make it airtight.

Leave it in a cool, dark room (around 18-20°C). The brine should rise to cover the cabbage within 24 hours. If it doesn't, add 1 tsp of sea salt with 200ml of water. Remove the weights.

Let it ferment for 3-5 days, pressing the cabbage down if it floats above the brine. Release any gasses that bubble up and skim off any scum. Taste the kraut after 3 days. It will get more sour the longer it ferments, so when you like the flavour, transfer it to a sterilised jar.

Once the Kraut is in its sterilised jar, store in the fridge for up to 6 months.

How to Use It

Serve alongside hearty meat stews or creamy pasta dishes to help cut through the richness.

Pile up on hot, buttered toast, or add to your favourite sandwich.

Fold through lentils, rice or toss with Asian-style noodles.

Mix into salads – it's especially delicious with watercress and/or freshly grated roots.

Try This

Carrot & Cabbage Krautchi, page 18

Rice

You can transform almost any humble veg into a delicious, nutritious 'rice' and it's a brilliant way to cut back on carbs and get more veg into your diet.

You don't need any fancy kit either. A food processor is the fastest route to ricing your veg, but you can just use a grater, or a knife and a chopping board.

Firm root veg and flowering brassicas work best. Think carrots, beetroot, sweet potatoes, butternut squash, kohlrabi, celeriac, broccoli and cauliflower.

How To

Peel if using root veg. Roughly chop. Pulse in a food processor, grate with a box grater or finely chop until it all looks a bit like rice or couscous.

Go raw and season it up with salt, pepper and a bit of spice if you like. Or fry the rice in an oiled pan with seasoning and herbs till steamy and tender. It only takes a few mins (the larger the pan, the faster it'll cook). Add a splash of water, if needed, to help it soften. To serve, use as a bed for curries, stir-fries, tagines and more, or dish it up (hot or cold) as a salad or a luscious side.

Combos

Broccoli fried up with coriander and cumin seeds.

Beetroot with a hint of chilli.

Carrot with lemon zest and fresh thyme.

Sweet potato with rosemary and a pinch of smoked paprika.

Cauliflower with orange zest and black pepper.

Try These

Za'atar Bazaar, page 15

Celeriac Couscous, page 219

Whip

You don't need an ice cream maker to whip up these fruity ice cream numbers.

Strawberries, blueberries, cherries, peaches, nectarines, apricots, plums, bananas, apples and pears all work a treat.

How To

The riper the fruit, the better. Just trim off any stems, pluck out the seeds or stones, roughly chop and freeze till firm.

For an extra touch of luxury without adding cream, try yogurt, cow's milk, coconut milk or almond milk. Full-fat options give best results.

For added sweetness, a dusting of icing sugar or a drop of honey or maple syrup work best. Caster sugar can be a little gritty as it won't dissolve.

And for a finishing touch, be playful! Add a little cinnamon, cardamom, star anise, a hint of coffee, some nuts, fresh herbs like basil or lemon verbena. The possibilities are almost endless...

Just blend your frozen fruit in a food processor or blender till it starts to resemble sorbet, trickle in the cream (or substitute), sweetener and flavourings as you blend. You should use approximately 1-2 tbsp of cream, 1-2 tsp of sweetener and a pinch of flavouring per mug of fruit.

Combos

Strawberry + coconut milk + icing sugar + rose water

Peaches + cream + maple syrup + cinnamon

Cherries + vanilla yogurt

Bananas + cold coffee + a splash of milk or cream + walnuts + cardamom

Try These

Kiwi Sorbet, page 49

Nectarine Ice, page 104

Cherry & Amaretto Ripple Ice Cream, page 109

Lemon & Pear Sorbet, page 196

Griddle

You don't need a barbecue to give your veggies a kiss of char-griddled greatness. You don't even need a fancy griddle pan. We use a frying pan as the veg gets more direct contact with the heat, and more char-griddled flavour.

You can griddle just about any fruit or veg. These are some favourites: spring onions, courgettes, aubergines, peppers, tomatoes, peaches, nectarines, plums, lettuce and leeks.

How To

Get your pan smoking hot. Prep your fruit or veg: leave smaller veg whole, slice big veg into panels. Dust with sea salt. Add the fruit or veg to the smoking hot pan. Cook without any oil: if your pan is smoking hot, the fruit or veg will form a crust, which will keep it from sticking. Cook on all sides till nicely charred.

Once you've griddled your fruit or veg, toss into salads or let them star as the main event. Dust with spices, herbs, cheese, toasted nuts or seeds, a hint of citrus and/or a gloss of oil.

Combos

Griddled peaches + basil + mozzarella

Griddled tomatoes blitzed with garlic, lime, cumin, paprika, salt and chilli for a smoky salsa

Griddled spring onions + scrambled eggs + feta on toasted sourdough

Griddled aubergine wedges brushed with a 50/50 mix of miso and honey and a little fresh ginger

Try These

Griddled Cabbage Steaks with Feta & Mint, page 21

Magic Miso & Sesame Dressing, page 33

Charred French Beans with Peanut & Tahini Dressing, page 84

Griddled Courgettes with Turmeric & Pickled Chilli, page 100

Pickle

Pickles are not only delicious, they're a brilliant way to tackle food waste. Anytime you've got a fruit or veggie on the turn, dunk them in our quick pickle brine and suddenly they go from goner to gourmet.

How To

Simply whisk together: 350ml of vinegar, 125ml of water and about 2 tbsp of honey, sugar or agave syrup. This will make brine for 2-3 jars.

Add character to your pickle witih some spice (mustard seeds, cinnamon sticks, cardamom pods, star anise, dried chillies and more), or fresh herbs like tarragon, dill or rosemary.

Carrots, plums, fennel, radishes, cauliflower, cucumbers, apples, cabbage, celery, pears, onions, leeks, spring onions, cherry tomatoes, courgettes, mushrooms, beetroot, chillies or summer stone fruits are just a few seasonal gems you can turn into pickles. Slice, dice, julienne (matchstick) or grate before pickling.

To make a quick pickle you can eat within minutes of making, simple heat the brine till warm. Swirl in your veg. Simmer for 1-2 mins. Take off the heat. Eat when ready. Or pile into sterilised jars (page 114) and store in the fridge for 1-2 weeks.

To make pickles that will keep, place the veg in a glass bowl with a generous dusting of salt. Let them sit overnight. Drain and rinse the veg. Pile into sterilised jars (page 114). Warm the brine (for long-life pickles, use a vinegar with acidity of 5 per cent or more) till just boiling. Pour over the veg till covering and the liquid comes right to the top. Secure lids. Store in a dry, cool place for up to 6 months.

Combos

Courgettes (ribbons or coarsely grated) + pinch of red chilli, mustard seeds and cumin + enough ground turmeric to give it a golden hue. Use cider vinegar as a base for the brine.

Cherry tomatoes (halved) + 2 or 3 tarragon sprigs + a white wine vinegar brine.

Apples or pears (thinly sliced) + a few slices of fresh ginger + 1 whole star anise and a cider vinegar brine.

Beetroot (coarsely grated) + a few strips of orange zest + 5 or 6 juniper berries in a balsamic vinegar brine.

Try These

Quickle Pickle Carrots, Labneh & Pistou, page 17

Quick Pickled Rhubarb, page 60

Preserved Bergamot Lemons, page 227

Dry

Dried fruit and veg make wonderful gifts and it's an ace way to celebrate bumper harvests. Drying also intensifies the flavour.

Clementines, all citrus zest, courgettes, aubergines, apples, mushrooms, herbs, leeks, beetroot and tomatoes are just some of the things you can dry.

How To

Slice your fruit or veg as thinly as possible. Halve or quarter tomatoes, then sprinkle with a little salt. Herbs can be left whole or finely chopped. Citrus zest can be finely grated or zested. For apples, squeeze over lemon juice to stop them browning. You can use your oven, or the warmth of the sun.

For the oven, line a baking tray with baking paper. Put your prepped fruit or veg in a single layer. Preheat your oven to 50°C/Gas 0 (lowest possible!). Bake the fruit/veg for 1 hr. Turn the oven off and leave your veg overnight to finish drying. Store in a container for up to one year.

Tomatoes need more heat than most veg. Cook at 110°C/Gas ¼ for 2–3 hrs till most of the moisture is gone (they'll be semi-dried). Pack in sterilised jars (page 114). Cover with oil. Seal and store in a cool place for up to 6 months.

Courgettes and aubergines: slice as thinly as possible and sprinkle with salt. Set a dry frying pan over a high heat. Once it's smoking hot, add the veg. Cook till charred on both sides. Pack in jars as above.

Hey sunshine, if you're going electricity-free, line a baking tray with a clean tea towel. Arrange your fruit, veg or herbs in a single layer and set in a warm, dry place untill fully dried. Herbs are best dried this way.

How to Use

Dried clementines are stunning added to mulled wine.

Use dried leeks and mushrooms in soups, stews and risottos.

Dried tomatoes and courgettes make a perfect party nibble or sandwich filling.

Try This

Mushroom Pot Noodle, page 252

Author Biographies

Rachel de Thample is the author of *Less Meat, More Veg* and *Five*. She has worked in the kitchens of Marco Pierre White, Heston Blumenthal and Peter Gordon and currently teaches the preserve courses at River Cottage HQ on the Dorset/Devon border. Rachel was Head of Fantastic Food for Abel & Cole for nearly 10 years. She lives in Crystal Palace, London, where she has helped set up numerous local food initiatives.

Jassy Davis is a food writer with a deep love for fresh, honest, natural foods. She trained at Ballymaloe in Ireland, a cookery school built on an organic farm. She recreated that experience at an inner city farm in London, setting up a café. She is the co-author of *The Contented Calf Cookbook*, *We Love Kale* and *We Love Quinoa*. She has written for publications including *lovefood.com* and *Huffington Post*; and is the lead recipe and product developer for Abel & Cole.

Sorrel Scott Blackmore is a food writer and experienced cook. Vegetables have always been at the root of her work within the food industry. Highlights include curating and cooking vegetarian feasts at the Garden Museum, catering for her own garden-inspired wedding, and collaborating with a number of renowned chefs. Sorrel was instrumental in the running of Sarah Raven's cookery school and cooked for intimate events and festivals at Perch Hill and Sissinghurst. She worked closely on Sarah's latest book *Good Good Food*. Sorrel currently works as a recipe developer and food stylist for Abel & Cole.

Gary Congress is an Australian-born photographer who loves to shoot anything to do with food. He had his first camera at the age of nine, which is about the same time he cooked his first bowl of spaghetti 'with ketchup'. He's been the in-house photographer at Abel & Cole for the past 10 years, and involved in their two previous cookbooks, *The Abel & Cole Veg Box Companion* and *The Abel & Cole Cookbook* and worked on many other food editorials and projects over the years. He lives in London with his wife, Lou, and their children, Sukie and Dexter.

Acknowledgements

So very many wonderful people have helped bring this book to life.

To start with, we are eternally thankful for all our amazing farmers, makers and bakers who genuinely inspire us every single day. Through their incredible hard work and care they make cooking and eating brilliantly possible. Particular thanks go to Berkeley Farm Dairy, Cocoa Loco, Albury Vineyard, Wross the Forager, Mole End Farm and Bagthorpe Farm - who all feature in this book in some way or another.

A very large serving of thanks must be offered to everyone in the Abel & Cole community - from our truly fantastic customers, to the legends who work tirelessly behind the scenes to get each and every string-tied box of organic food designed, planned, packed and delivered - and everyone in between.

Finally, many of the Abel & Cole bunch have lent their time, energy and wisdom to add dashes of sparkle and joy to this book. Lashings of thanks to some of our (now) extended family, who have lent us beautiful locations, helped with photoshoots and generally given their time and thoughts to creating this book, which was very enjoyable to work on.

So a HUGE thank you goes to:

Abel & Cole
Jocelyn Grant
Emma Stringer
Barry Lattimore-Quinn
Claudia Ruane
Matt Crossland
Fred Mackenzie
Hannah Shipton
Pippa Bridle
Lily Thompson

Further afield
Lydia Good
Lawrence Morton
Esther Clark
Harriet Worthington
Iris Borger (and her team at Grow Mayow, a great little community garden in Sydenham, where we shot the glorious summer chapter)

Index

A

Abel & 'Bena 128
Abel & Cole
    history 6
    the Abel & Cole way 8
Abel, Keith 6
Amour Tatin Tomate 93
anchovies 38, 78, 207, 212
apples 156, 208, 223
    Collina 156
    Discovery 156
    Egremont Russet 156
    Falstaff 156
    Fiesta 156
    Galas 156
    Parsnip & Apple Pancakes 216
    Red Windsor 156
    Roast Toffee Apples 160
    Saturn 156
    Spartan 156
    West Country Quiche 158
    Winter Waldorf Soup 167
Apricot Bellinis 124
asparagus
    Asparagus & Egg-fried Quinoa 28
    Asparagus & Mint Pesto 61
    Asparagus Benedict Royale 29
    Crispy Buckwheat with Saffron
        Yogurt & Asparagus 30
    Magic Miso & Sesame Dressing 33
    Asparagus & Egg-fried Quinoa 28
    Asparagus & Mint Pesto 61
    Asparagus Benedict Royale 29
    A Game of Tagine 154
aubergine
    Mediterranean Aubergine & Herb
        Salad 121
    preparing 121, 122
    Smoky Aubergine & Tahini
        Chocolate Brownies 122
    Tahini Aubergine Wedges 131
    Autumn 132-197
avocado 38, 51, 250
    Chilled-out Lemon, Lettuce &
        Avocado Soup 76
    Matcha of Day 193
    Smoothie in a Jar'O 51

B

bacon 144, 181
    Bacon & Sage Frittata with Warm
        Cannellini Bean Salad 145
    dry curing 144
Bacon & Sage Frittata with Warm
    Cannellini Bean Salad 145
Baked Golden Beetroot Risotto with
    Roasted Garlic Cream 235
bananas
    Bananas About Macaroons 48
    Banana & Peanut Butter Mousse 60

Golden Milkshake 51
Matcha of Day 193
Smoothie in a Jar'O 51
Bananas About Macaroons 48
Banana & Peanut Butter Mousse 60
Barbecued Watermelon, Feta & Walnut
    Salad 103
beetroot 247
    Baked Golden Beetroot Risotto with
        Roasted Garlic Cream 235
    Bombay Beetroot Salad 232
    Cumin Beet & Orange Carpaccio 253
blackberries
    Abel & 'Bena 128
    blackcurrants
    Abel & 'Bena 128
Blood Orange Piri Piri Chicken 224
Bombay Beetroot Salad 232
bread 57
    No-knead Slow-fermentation
        Bread 185
    The Authentic Bread Company 57
brine 18
broad beans
    Popping Summer Bean Energy
        Salad 69
    Whipped Minted Broad Beans 66
    Wonderful One-Pot Summer
        Spaghetti 65
broccoli
    Broccoli Slaw with Red Thai Yogurt &
        Toasted Cashews 140
    Broccoli Walnut Rarebit 143
    Grilled PSB Satay 42
    purple sprouting 42
    tenderstem 42
    Broccoli Slaw with Red Thai Yogurt &
        Toasted Cashews 140
    Broccoli Walnut Rarebit 143
broth
    how to serve it 259
    making 259
Browning, Helen 106
Brussels sprouts
    Coconut & Chilli Sprouts 253
    buckwheat
Crispy Buckwheat with Saffron Yogurt &
    Asparagus 30
Butter-roasted Sweetcorn 135
Butterscotch & Parsnip Pud 244

C

cabbage 18, 22, 24-5, 232
    Caraway Cabbage Noodles 61
    Carrot & Cabbage Krautchi 18
    Ciderrrr Buttered Greens 22
    Green pointed 24
    Griddled Cabbage Steaks with Feta
        & Mint 21
    January King 24

Rumbledethumps 172
Savoy 24
Spring Greens 24
Tundra 24
Caesar Royals 78
cannellini beans
    Bacon & Sage Frittata with Warm
        Cannellini Bean Salad 145
Caraway Cabbage Noodles 61
carbon sinks 200
Cardamom, Walnut & Pear Chicken 178
Carrot & Cabbage Krautchi 18
carrots 15, 26, 232
    Carrot & Cabbage Krautchi 18
    Carrot-top Seaweed 60
    Carroty Carrot Cookies 54
    Jive Time Carrot Mash & Coriander
        Pesto 14
    Quickle Pickle Carrots, Labneh &
        Pistou 17
    Za'atar Bazaar 15
Carrot-top Seaweed 60
Carroty Carrot Cookies 54
Cashew, Turmeric & Date Dressing 211
cauliflower
    Cobb Salad 155
    Ginger Wok Cauliflower 197
    head-to-stalk eating 153
    Jolly Roast Cauli 153
    Roast Cauli & Cashew Biryani 150
    Southern-fried Cauli 155
cavolo nero 217
celeriac
    Celeriac Couscous 219
    Celeriac Noodles with Mushroom
        Pesto 221
    Celeriac Soup with a Zesty Kick 220
Celeriac Noodles with Mushroom Pesto
    221
Celeriac Soup with a Zesty Kick 220
celery 26, 167
Charred French beans with Peanut &
    Tahini Dressing 84
Cheddar
    Amour Tatin Tomate 93
    Broccoli Walnut Rarebit 143
    Rumbledethumps 172
    West Country Quiche 158
cherries 109
    Cherry & Amaretto Ripple Ice Cream
        109
Cherry & Amaretto Ripple Ice Cream 109
chicken
    Blood Orange Piri Piri Chicken 224
    Cardamom, Walnut & Pear Chicken 178
    organic chickens 224
    Perfect Poached Chicken & Wild
        Garlic Gremolata Broth 26
chickpeas 96

Chilled-out Lemon, Lettuce & Avocado
     Soup 76
Chipped New Potatoes 81
chocolate 56
     Chocolate Cloud Biscuits 191
     Fantastic Frozen Strawberries with
          Warm White Choc & Cardamom
          Sauce 113
     Jewelled Chocolate Torte 242
     Red Velvet Truffles 247
     Smoky Aubergine & Tahini
          Chocolate Brownies 122
     Spiced Gingerbread Truffles 248
     White Choc Passion Puds 58
Chocolate Cloud Biscuits 191
Ciderrrr Buttered Greens 22
Cobb Salad 155
coconut 51
     Bananas About Macaroons 48
     Coconut & Chilli Sprouts 253
     Coconut-creamed Kale 253
     Golden Milkshake 51
     Sunny Spiced Courgette & Coconut
          Soup 99
     Swede & Coconut Daal 171
Coconut & Chilli Sprouts 253
Coconut-creamed Kale 253
Coconut Sugar Caramel Blood
     Oranges 246
courgetti
     cooking 65, 94
     Courgette & Mint Polpette 96
     Ginger & Tomato Baked Cod with
          Lime Courgetti 94
     Wonderful One-Pot Summer
          Spaghetti 65
Crab Apple Whisky 195
Crispy Buckwheat with Saffron Yogurt &
     Asparagus 30
cucumber 103
Cumin Beet & Orange Carpaccio 253

D
dates 244, 248
     A Game of Tagine 154
     Cashew, Turmeric & Date Dressing 211
Dickensian Gammon 208
drinks
     Abel & 'Bena 128
     Apricot Bellinis 124
     Crab Apple Whisky 195
     Elderflower & Strawberry Power
          Pressé 126
     Ginger Melon Smoothie 124
     Golden Milkshake 51
     Gooseberry Lemonade 128
     Juiced Rubies 250
     Matcha of Day 193
     non-alcoholic drinks 52, 124
     Pear & Rosemary G&T 194
     Popeye Pears 193
     Rhuby G&T 52
     Smoothie in a Jar'O 51
     Spiced Ale Flip 250
drying

combos 265
making 265

E
eating seasonally 10
     see also seasonal swaps 10
     see also seasonal stars 13
eggs 228-9
     Asparagus & Egg-fried Quinoa 28
     Asparagus Benedict Royale 29
     Sweet & Sour Rhubarb Pork with Egg-
          fried Rice 41
     using leftover yolks 231
elderflowers
     Elderflower & Strawberry Power
          Pressé 126
     Elderflower Soaked Berries 130
Elderflower & Strawberry Power
     Pressé 126
Elderflower Soaked Berries 130
emergency substitutions 11

F
Fantastic Frozen Strawberries with
     Warm White Choc & Cardamom
     Sauce 113
Feisty Nectarine Relish 105
fennel 17, 38
     Hazelnut & Thyme's Greatest
          Gratin 164
feta 66
     Barbecued Watermelon, Feta &
          Walnut Salad 103
     Griddled Cabbage Steaks with Feta
          & Mint 21
     Pattypan Squash Stuffed with
          Sweetcorn & Feta 138
     whipped feta 239
fish 86
     Ginger & Tomato Baked Cod with
          Lime Courgetti 94
     Hake Burgers with Roast Garlic
          Mayo 88
     see also sustainable sourcing
     Spring Up Salmon Caesar 38
Flower Power Sprouts with Anchovy
     Dressing 207
foraging 9
     rules of 126
French beans
     Charred French Beans with Peanut &
          Tahini Dressing 84
     Green & Gold Potato Salad 83
Fresh Corn Polenta with Peperonata 137
Frittata 145
     Bacon & Sage Frittata with Warm
          Cannellini Bean Salad 145

G
gammon
     Dickensian Gammon 208
garlic, roasting 235
Gazza's Indian Hotpot 166
Ginger & Tomato Baked Cod with Lime
     Courgetti 94

Ginger Melon Smoothie 124
Ginger Sesame Leek Rice 239
Ginger Wok Cauliflower 197
goat's cheese 121
Golden Maple & Walnut Parsnips 205
Golden Milkshake 51
gooseberries 126
     Gooseberry Lemonade 128
Gooseberry Lemonade 128
Greek Slow-roast Hogget Shoulder 19
Green & Gold Potato Salad 83
green lentils 96

H
Hake Burgers with Roast Garlic Mayo 88
ham
     West Country Quiche 158
Haunch of Venison with Rosemary &
     Pear Stuffing 181
Hazelnut & Thyme's Greatest Gratin 164
hogget
     Greek Slow-roast Hogget Shoulder 19
Honeybear Pear Flapjacks 182
Honeyed Orange & Polenta Pancakes 231
Hot Dogs with Beer & Mustard Onions 106

J
Jersey Royals
     See new potatoes
Jewelled Chocolate Torte 242
Jive Time Carrot Mash & Coriander
     Pesto 14
Jolly Roast Cauli 153
Juiced Rubies 250

K
kale
     Coconut-creamed Kale 253
     Kale Pancakes with Tahini Butter 214
     Majestic Spiced Kale &
          Pomegranate 241
     Rumbledethumps 172
     Winter Salsa Verde 212
Kale Pancakes with Tahini Butter 214
kiwi fruits
     Kiwi Sorbet 49
     Korean Kiwi Dressing 45
Kiwi Sorbet 49
Korean Kiwi Dressing 45
kraut
     Carrot & Cabbage Krautchi 18
     how to use it 260
     making 18, 260

L
labneh 17
     making 17
     Quickle Pickle Carrots, Labneh &
          Pistou 17
lamb
     Greek Slow-roast Hogget Shoulder 19
lamb's lettuce 38
Late Summer Tricolore 186
leeks 150
     Ginger Sesame Leek Rice 239

Oak-smoked Leeks 236
Lemon & Pear Sorbet 196
lentils
Swede & Coconut Daal 171
lettuce 71
Lettuce Dippers 130
Lettuce Dippers 130
Lettuce Tartlettes 72

M
Magic Miso & Sesame Dressing 33
Majestic Spiced Kale & Pomegranate 241
mash
Combos 256
making 256
Matcha of Day 193
Mediterranean Aubergine & Herb
Salad 121
Melon Salad Bowl 131
Mexican Popping Sweetcorn 196
miso 33
Magic Miso & Sesame Dressing 33
mozzarella 186
mushrooms 145, 217
Celeriac Noodles with Mushroom
Pesto 221
Parsnip & Mushroom Pan Pie 204
Mushroom Pot Noodle 252
Mutton Mince Pie 223

N
Nectarine Ice 104
nectarines
Feisty Nectarine Relish 105
Grilled Nectarines with Amaretto
Mascarpone 130
Nectarine Ice 104
new potatoes 29
Asparagus Benedict Royale 29
Caesar Royals 78
Chipped New Potatoes 81
Green & Gold Potato Salad 83
No-knead Slow-fermentation Bread 185

O
Oak-smoked Leeks 236
oranges 41, 186, 191
Blood Orange Piri Piri Chicken 224
Coconut Sugar Caramel Blood
Oranges 246
Cumin Beet & Orange Carpaccio 253
Honeyed Orange & Polenta
Pancakes 231
organic
farming 6, 7, 8, 111
food 7, 8

P
Parsnip & Apple Pancakes 216
Parsnip & Blue Cheese Gratin 202
Parsnip & Mushroom Pan Pie 204
Parsnip, Hazelnut & Sage Hash 252
parsnips
Butterscotch & Parsnip Pud 244

Golden Maple & Walnut Parsnips 205
Parsnip & Apple Pancakes 216
Parsnip & Blue Cheese Gratin 202
Parsnip & Mushroom Pan Pie 204
Parsnip, Hazelnut & Sage Hash 252
passionfruit 58
pastry 46, 72, 93, 154, 158, 189, 223
sprouted spelt 46
Pattypan Squash Stuffed with
Sweetcorn & Feta 138
pea shoots 65
peanut butter
Banana & Peanut Butter Mousse 60
Charred French Beans with Peanut &
Tahini Dressing 84
Grilled PSB Satay 42
pear
Cardamom, Walnut & Pear Chicken 178
Haunch of Venison with Rosemary &
Pear Stuffing 181
Honeybear Pear Flapjacks 182
Lemon & Pear Sorbet 196
Pear & Rosemary G&T 194
Popeye Pears 193
Pear & Rosemary G&T 194
Perfect Poached Chicken & Wild Garlic
Gremolata Broth 26
Persian Pomegranate pots 252
pheasants 171
pickling
carrots 17
combos 264
making 264
Plum & Bay Custard Tart 189
Plummy Pork Chops 196
plums
Late Summer Tri colore 186
Plum & Bay Custard Tart 189
Plummy Pork Chops 196
Sugar Plums 190
pomegranate
Jewelled Chocolate Torte 242
Juiced Rubies 250
Majestic Spiced Kale &
Pomegranate 241
Persian Pomegranate pots 252
releasing seeds, 241
Squash & Tahini Soup with
Pomegranate 149
Popeye Pears 193
Popping Summer Bean Energy Salad 69
pork
Plummy Pork Chops 196
Sweet & Sour Rhubarb Pork with Egg-
fried Rice 41
potatoes 163
Anya 163
Arran Victory 163
Athlete 163
Bambino 163
Dickensian Gammon 208
Estima 163
Gazza's Indian Hotpot 166
Hazelnut & Thyme's Greatest Gratin
164

Milva 163
Orla 163
Parsnip & Blue Cheese Gratin 202
Rudolph 163
Rumbledethumps 172
Winter Waldorf Soup 167
Preserved Bergamot Lemons 227
preserving 9, 114, 227
Preserved Bergamot Lemons
227
Strawberry & Prosecco Jam 114
Pulled Pumpkin 146
Pumpkin & Chorizo Hash 197
pumpkin and squashes
Pattypan Squash Stuffed with
Sweetcorn & Feta 138
Pulled Pumpkin 146
Pumpkin & Chorizo Hash 197
Squash & Tahini Soup with
Pomegranate 149
Squash Cauldron 154

Q
Quick Pickled Rhubarb 60
Quickle Pickle Carrots, Labneh &
Pistou 17
quinoa 28
Asparagus & Egg-fried Quinoa 28

R
Radish Top & Walnut Pesto 61
radishes 37
Radish Top & Walnut Pesto 61
Salt & Butter-cracked Radishes 37
Spring Up Salmon Caesar 38
red pepper 15, 121, 153
Fresh Corn Polenta with Peperonata
137
Red Velvet Truffles 247
rhubarb 41
preparing rhubarb 41
Quick Pickled Rhubarb 60
Rhuby G&T 52
Rhuby, Thyme, Lime & Almond
Tart 46
Sweet & Sour Rhubarb Pork with Egg-
fried Rice 41
Rhuby G&T 52
Rhuby, Thyme, Lime & Almond Tart 46
rice
combos 261
making 261
Roast Cauli & Cashew Biryani 150
Roast Toffee Apples 160
rocket 186
romaine lettuce
Griddled Romaine & Minted Tahini
Yogurt Sauce 73
Rumbledethumps 172

S
salads
Bombay Beetroot Salad 232
Mediterranean Aubergine & Herb
Salad 121

Melon Salad Bowl 131
Spring Up Salmon Caesar 38
Za'atar Bazaar 15
Salt & Butter-cracked Radishes 37
sauces and dressings
Anchovy Dressing 207
Asparagus & Mint Pesto 61
butter 29
Buttermilk Dressing 155
Caesar dressing 78
Cardamom Sauce 113
Cashew, Turmeric & Date Dressing 211
Gremolata 95
Grilled PSB Satay 42
Korean Kiwi Dressing 45
Minted Tahini Yogurt Sauce 73
Piri Piri Sauce 224
Red Thai Yogurt 140
Roast Garlic Mayo 88
Saffron Yogurt 30
Sesame Dressing 33
Tahini dressing 84
Tahini yogurt 131
THE Sauce 91
Warm White Choc & Cardamom
Sauce 113
Winter Salsa Verde 212
sausages
Hot Dogs with Beer & Mustard
Onions 106
Summer Bangers with Gremolata 95
slaw
Broccoli Slaw with Red Thai Yogurt &
Toasted Cashews 140
combos 257
making 257
smoking
combos 258
making 257
Smoky Aubergine & Tahini Chocolate
Brownies 122
Smoothie in a Jar'O 51
soil, organic 174
Soil Association 106
soups
Celeriac Soup with a Zesty Kick 220
Chilled-out Lemon, Lettuce &
Avocado Soup 76
Jive Time Carrot Mash & Coriander
Pesto 14
Perfect Poached Chicken & Wild
Garlic Gremolata Broth 26
Squash & Tahini Soup with
Pomegranate 149
Sunny Spiced Courgette & Coconut
Soup 99
Winter Waldorf Soup 167
Southern-fried Cauli 155
Spiced Ale Flip 250
Spiced Gingerbread Truffles 248
spinach 51, 145, 150, 193
Spring 12-61
spring greens 22, 24
Ciderrrr Buttered Greens 22
spring onions 28, 33, 41

Spring Up Salmon Caesar 38
Squash & Tahini Soup with
Pomegranate 149
Squash Cauldron 154
sterilising jars 114
Store Cupboard Swaps 10
strawberries 126
Elderflower & Strawberry Power
Pressé 126
Fantastic Frozen Strawberries with
Warm White Choc & Cardamom
Sauce 113
Strawberry & Prosecco Jam 114
Strawberry Cheesecake Yogurt 116
Strawberry & Prosecco Jam 114
Strawberry Cheesecake Yogurt 116
Sugar Plums 190
sugar snap peas 69
Popping Summer Bean Energy
Salad 69
Summer 62-131
Summer Bangers with Gremolata 95
Sunny Spiced Courgette & Coconut
Soup 99
sustainable sourcing 9, 86
swede
Rumbledethumps 172
Swede & Coconut Daal 171
Swedish Roast Swede 197
Swede & Coconut Daal 171
Swedish Roast Swede 197
Sweet & Sour Rhubarb Pork with Egg-
fried Rice 41
sweet potato 154
sweetcorn
Butter-roasted Sweetcorn 135
Fresh Corn Polenta with Peperonata
137
Mexican Popping Sweetcorn 196
Pattypan Squash Stuffed with
Sweetcorn & Feta 138

T
tahini
Charred French Beans with Peanut &
Tahini Dressing 84
Griddled Romaine & Minted Tahini
Yogurt Sauce 73
Kale Pancakes with Tahini Butter 214
Smoky Aubergine & Tahini
Chocolate Brownies 122
Squash & Tahini Soup with
Pomegranate 149
Tahini Aubergine Wedges 131
Tahini Aubergine Wedges 131
testing for setting point 114
The Authentic Bread Company 57
THE Sauce 91
Tomato Dip Dabs 131
Tomatoes 154
Amour Tatin Tomate 93
cherry 30, 65, 93, 95, 137, 145
Ginger & Tomato Baked Cod with
Lime Courgetti 94
THE Sauce 91

Tomato Dip Dabs 131

U
unhomogenised milk 34

V
venison 217
Haunch of Venison with Rosemary &
Pear Stuffing 181
Winter Woodland Dolmades 217
vintners and organic wine 119

W
walnuts 54, 217, 223, 244
Barbecued Watermelon, Feta &
Walnut Salad 103
Broccoli Walnut Rarebit 143
Cardamom, Walnut & Pear
Chicken 178
Celeriac Noodles with Mushroom
Pesto 221
Golden Maple & Walnut Parsnips 205
Radish Top & Walnut Pesto 61
Winter Waldorf Soup 167
watercress 65
watermelon
Barbecued Watermelon, Feta &
Walnut Salad 103
Watermelon Mojito Lollies 125
Watermelon Mojito Lollies 125
West Country Quiche 158
whip
combos 262
making 262
Whipped Minted Broad Beans 66
White Choc Passion Puds 58
wild garlic
Perfect Poached Chicken & Wild
Garlic Gremolata Broth 26
Winter 198-253
Winter Salsa Verde 212
Winter Waldorf Soup 167
Winter Woodland Dolmades 217
Wonderful One-Pot Summer Spaghetti 65

Y
Yogurt 155
Broccoli Slaw with Red Thai Yogurt &
Toasted Cashews 140
Crispy Buckwheat with Saffron
Yogurt & Asparagus 30
Quickle Pickle Carrots, Labneh &
Pistou 17
Red Thai Yogurt 140
Strawberry Cheesecake Yogurt 116
Tahini Yogurt Sauce 73
Yogurt pastry 154

Z
Za'atar Bazaar 15

13579108642

Ebury Press, an imprint of Ebury Publishing,
20 Vauxhall Bridge Road,
London SW1V 2SA

Ebury Press is part of the Penguin Random House group of companies
whose addresses can be found at global.penguinrandomhouse.com

Penguin
Random House
UK

Text by Rachel de Thample, Jassy Davis, Sorrel Scott

Photography by Gary Congress, with additional field shots by Fred Mackenzie

Food styling: Rachel de Thample, Jassy Davis, Sorrel Scott, Esther Clark, Harriet Worthington

Design: Lawrence Morton

Editor: Lydia Good

First published by Ebury Press in 2017

www.eburypublishing.co.uk

A CIP catalogue record for this book is available from the British Library

ISBN 9781785035791

Printed and bound in Italy by L.E.G.O. S.p.A